CAST OF CHARACTERS

Common People in the Hands of an Uncommon God

MAX LUCADO

THOMAS NELSON
Since 1798

NASHVILLE   DALLAS   MEXICO CITY   RIO DE JANEIRO   BEIJING

Published in Nashville, Tennessee, by Thomas Nelson. Thomas Nelson is a registered trademark of Thomas Nelson, Inc.

ISBN 978-0-8499-2124-7

Printed in the United States of America

For Landon Saunders

I'm still warmed by your words and grateful for your smile.

ALSO BY MAX LUCADO

CONTENTS

INTRODUCTION

Sitting at the sidewalk cafe table next to yours is a young man, twenty-ish, dark hair. His dress suggests working class; sinewy muscles and sunned skin imply outdoor work. Lawn maintenance? Carpentry? You don't mean to stare . . . but he has a different look to him. His complexion and facial features tag him as foreign. You don't mean to stare, but before you can stop, he notices and smiles.

"I'm Hebrew."

"Sorry?"

"You're not the first to wonder about me. I'm Hebrew. Only been in Egypt a couple of years."

You shift your chair in his direction and lean forward. "What brought you here?"

"Might I give the short version?"

You nod and he begins.

"Well, my father tricked my uncle out of his inheritance. Of course, Grandma wanted my father to swindle my uncle. She was the brains behind the ploy. Uncle Esau, so angry at being suckered, decided to kill my father. Dad escaped with the shirt on his back and his head on his shoulders and was happy to have that. He found refuge in my great-uncle's family. Perhaps you've heard of Laban? Of course you haven't. No reason you would have, except that he had a good spread of livestock back where I came from. Anyway, Dad fell in love with one of his daughters and, by accident, married a different one. Laban tricked the trickster. Seems my aunt was too homey looking to land a man, so Laban landed one for her. Dad eventually married Mom. She was his favorite, you know. But she was slow to get pregnant, so he had a clan of kids with other women, one of whom was my mother's sister. The homey-looking one. By the time I came along, the house was swarming with children. But I was his favorite. He gave me gifts and attention that the others never received. Left them jealous as hornets. They sold me to slave traders, and I ended up here in Egypt. Dad must think I'm dead. But I'm not. I am hungry, however. Plan on finishing that humus?"

You hand him your plate and stare as he spoons it clean and wonder what kind of story this might be. Scoundrels scamming deceivers. Cheats misleading two-timers. What kind of people are these? Exactly the kind who comprise God's cast of characters. Joseph and his family are just a few of the hoi polloi and ne'er-do-wells whose stories form the stuff of Scripture. Jacob highjacking Esau at the behest of their mother, Rebekah. Uncle Laban pulling a honeymoon switcheroo so slick that Jacob didn't know he'd married the wrong woman until the morning after the vows had been made and the cake cut. Joseph strutting around like the proud peacock, infuriating the very brothers who became the namesakes for the twelve tribes of Israel and cardholding members of the family tree of Jesus. Yes, Jesus Christ!

Climb up his family tree and you'll find worm-infested apples. It's all laid out in the first chapter of the New Testament. Matthew lists forty-two relatives, all of whom have questionable character. Got time for a few examples?

- One of his great-grandmothers played the harlot in hopes of swindling Judah (a brother of Joseph) into keeping his word.
- Another of the great-grandmothers didn't have to play the harlot. She was one, presiding as madam over an unpretentious little place in the red-light district of Jericho.
- Bathsheba was a tabloid mainstay—the bathing beauty who found her way into Scripture via the arms of King David.
- And David. The giant killer who couldn't corral his testosterone. The guy had more wives than common sense.

- His son Solomon had both wives and cents; financial cents, that is. Has any king been so rich and so lonely? "Vanity of vanities" they carved on his headstone.

The ancestors of Jesus. Story after story marked by scandal, stumble, and intrigue. Who are these people?

Us. That's who they are.

We find our stories in theirs. We find our hope where they found theirs. In the midst of them all . . . hovering over them all . . . is the hero of it all: God. Maker. Shaper. Rescuer of sinking hearts. God. Passing out high callings, second chances, and moral compasses to all comers and takers. To Moses—who murdered; Samson—who slipped; Thomas—who second-guessed God; to John the Baptist—who dressed like a caveman and had the diet of a grizzly bear.

These are the people of the Bible, brimming with much more spunk and spark than many people realize. I love to read their stories. Through the years I've even taken a stab at retelling a few of them. This book is a collection of some of those efforts. Let me thank Laura Kendall, Karen Hill, and Andrea Lucado for managing the harvest. Thanks also to David Moberg and the Thomas Nelson team for suggesting the idea.

We offer these pages to you on the wings of a wonderful promise: if God can find a place for these characters . . . he just might have a place for us too. A jewel of a verse from the book of Hebrews implies as much.

Jesus, who makes people holy, and those who are made holy are from the same family. So he is not ashamed to call them his brothers and sisters. He says, . . . "I am here, and with me are the children God has given me." (Hebrews 2:11–13)

The passage has the feel of a family reunion photo. An assemblage of aunts, uncles, cousins, and kin, gathered for a wedding, summer picnic, or holiday. All the curious characters of the family are present. A drifter, a drunk, the uncle who never grew up, and the aunt who never shuts up. The cousin with the police record and the grandpa with the salty language. Joseph in his Egyptian garb and his father, Jacob, with the darting eyes. Uncle Laban and King David. Everyone is here—including Jesus. He sits smack dab in the middle of them, smiling like the proud papa he is. "I am here, and with me are the children God has given me."

Do you see your face in the photo? I hope you do . . . you're in it. And he's proud of you too.

chapter one

JOSEPH

This is how the birth of Jesus Christ came about. His mother Mary was engaged to marry Joseph, but before they married, she learned she was pregnant by the power of the Holy Spirit. Because Mary's husband, Joseph, was a good man, he did not want to disgrace her in public, so he planned to divorce her secretly.

While Joseph thought about these things, an angel of the Lord came to him in a dream. The angel said, "Joseph, descendant of David, don't be afraid to take Mary as your wife, because the baby in her is from the Holy Spirit. She will give birth to a son, and you will name him Jesus, because he will save his people from their sins."

All this happened to bring about what the Lord had said through the prophet: "The virgin will be pregnant. She will have a son, and they will name him Immanuel," which means "God is with us."

When Joseph woke up, he did what the Lord's angel had told him to do. Joseph took Mary as his wife, but he did not have sexual relations with her until she gave birth to the son. And Joseph named him Jesus.

{ MATT. 1:18–25 }

JOSEPH'S PRAYER

The white space between Bible verses is fertile soil for questions. One can hardly read Scripture without whispering, "I wonder . . ."

"I wonder if Eve ever ate any more fruit."

"I wonder if Noah slept well during storms."

"I wonder if Jonah liked fish or if Jeremiah had friends."

"Did Moses avoid bushes? Did Jesus tell jokes? Did Peter ever try water-walking again?"

"Would any woman have married Paul had he asked?"

The Bible is a fence full of knotholes through which we can peek but not see the whole picture. It's a scrapbook of snapshots capturing people in encounters with God, but not always recording the result. A cast of characters in a drama of cosmic importance, but without a denouement. So we wonder:

When the woman caught in adultery went home, what did she say to her husband?

After the demoniac was delivered, what did he do for a living?

After Jairus's daughter was raised from the dead, did she ever regret it?

Knotholes and snapshots and "I wonders." You'll find them in every chapter about every person. But nothing stirs so many questions as does the birth of Christ. Characters appear and disappear before we can ask them anything. The innkeeper too busy to welcome God—did he ever learn who he turned away? The shepherds—did they ever hum the song the angels sang? The wise men who followed the star—what was it like to worship a toddler? And Joseph, especially Joseph. I've got questions for Joseph.

Did you and Jesus arm wrestle? Did he ever let you win?

3

Did you ever look up from your prayers and see Jesus listening?

How do you say "Jesus" in Egyptian?

What ever happened to the wise men?

What ever happened to you?

We don't know what happened to Joseph. His role in Act I is so crucial that we expect to see him the rest of the drama—but with the exception of a short scene with twelve-year-old Jesus in Jerusalem, he never reappears. The rest of his life is left to speculation, and we are left with our questions.

But of all my questions, my first would be about Bethlehem. I'd like to know about the night in the stable. I can picture Joseph there. Moonlit pastures. Stars twinkle above. Bethlehem sparkles in the distance. There he is, pacing outside the stable.

What was he thinking while Jesus was being born? What was on his mind while Mary was giving birth? He'd done all he could do—heated the water, prepared a place for Mary to lie. He'd made Mary as comfortable as she could be in a barn and then he stepped out. She'd asked to be alone, and Joseph has never felt more so.

In that eternity between his wife's dismissal and Jesus' arrival, what was he thinking? He walked into the night and looked into the stars. Did he pray?

For some reason, I don't see him silent; I see Joseph animated, pacing. Head shaking one minute, fist shaking the next. This isn't what he had in mind. I wonder what he said . . .

This isn't the way I planned it, God. Not at all. My child being born in a stable? This isn't the way I thought it would be. A cave with sheep and donkeys, hay and straw? My wife giving birth with only the stars to hear her pain?

This isn't at all what I imagined. No, I imagined family. I imagined grandmothers. I imagined neighbors clustered outside the door and friends standing at my side. I imagined the house erupting with the first cry of the infant. Slaps on the back. Loud laughter. Jubilation.

That's how I thought it would be.

The midwife would hand me my child and all the people would applaud. Mary would rest and we would celebrate. All of Nazareth would celebrate.

But now. Now look. Nazareth is five days' journey away. And here we are in a . . . in a sheep pasture. Who will celebrate with us? The sheep? The shepherds? The stars?

This doesn't seem right. What kind of husband am I? I provide no midwife to aid my wife. No bed to rest her back. Her pillow is a blanket from my donkey. My house for her is a shed of hay and straw.

The smell is bad, the animals are loud. Why, I even smell like a shepherd myself.

Did I miss something? Did I, God?

When you sent the angel and spoke of the son being born—this isn't what I pictured. I envisioned Jerusalem, the temple, the priests, and the people gathered to watch. A pageant perhaps. A parade. A banquet at least. I mean, this is the Messiah!

Or, if not born in Jerusalem, how about Nazareth? Wouldn't Nazareth have been better? At least there I have my house and my business. Out here, what do I have? A weary mule, a stack of firewood, and a pot of warm water. This is not the way I wanted it to be! This is not the way I wanted my son.

Oh my, I did it again. I did it again, didn't I, Father? I don't mean to do that; it's just that I forget. He's not my son . . . he's yours.

The child is yours. The plan is yours. The idea is yours. And forgive me for asking but . . . is this how God enters the world? The coming of the angel, I've accepted. The questions people asked about the pregnancy, I can tolerate. The trip to Bethlehem, fine. But why a birth in a stable, God?

Any minute now Mary will give birth. Not to a child, but to the Messiah. Not to an infant, but to God. That's what the angel said. That's what Mary believes. And, God, my God, that's what I want to believe. But surely you can understand; it's not easy. It seems so . . . so . . . so . . . bizarre.

I'm unaccustomed to such strangeness, God. I'm a carpenter. I make things fit. I square off the edges. I follow the plumb line. I measure twice before I cut once. Surprises are not the friend of a builder. I like to know the plan. I like to see the plan before I begin.

But this time I'm not the builder, am I? This time I'm a tool. A hammer in your grip. A nail between your fingers. A chisel in your hands. This project is yours, not mine.

I guess it's foolish of me to question you. Forgive my struggling. Trust doesn't come easy to me, God. But you never said it would be easy, did you?

One final thing, Father. The angel you sent? Any chance you could send another? If not an angel, maybe a person? I don't know anyone around here and some company would be nice. Maybe the innkeeper or a traveler? Even a shepherd would do.

I wonder. Did Joseph ever pray such a prayer? Perhaps he did. Perhaps he didn't.

But you probably have.

You've stood where Joseph stood. Caught between what God says and what makes sense. You've done what he told you to do only to wonder if it was him speaking in the first place. You've stared into a sky blackened with doubt. And you've asked what Joseph asked.

You've asked if you're still on the right road. You've asked if you were supposed to turn left when you turned right. And you've asked if there is a plan behind this scheme. Things haven't turned out like you thought they would.

Each of us knows what it's like to search the night for light. Not outside a stable, but perhaps outside an emergency room. On the gravel of a roadside. On the manicured grass of a cemetery. We've asked our questions. We questioned God's plan. And we've wondered why God does what he does.

The Bethlehem sky is not the first to hear the pleadings of a confused pilgrim.

If you are asking what Joseph asked, let me urge you to do what Joseph did. Obey. That's what he did. He obeyed. He obeyed when the angel called. He obeyed when Mary explained. He obeyed when God sent.

He was obedient to God.

He was obedient when the sky was bright.

He was obedient when the sky was dark.

He didn't let his confusion disrupt his obedience. He didn't know everything. But he did what he knew. He shut down his business, packed up his family, and went to another country. Why? Because that's what God said to do.

What about you? Just like Joseph, you can't see the whole picture. Just like Joseph your task is to see that Jesus is brought into your part of your world. And just like Joseph you have a choice: to obey or disobey. Because Joseph obeyed, God used him to change the world.

Can he do the same with you?

God still looks for Josephs today. Men and women who believe that God is not through with this world. Common people who serve an uncommon God.

Will you be that kind of person? Will you serve . . . even when you don't understand?

No, the Bethlehem sky is not the first to hear the pleadings of an honest heart, nor the last. And perhaps God didn't answer every question for Joseph. But he answered the most important one. "Are you still with me, God?" And through the first cries of the God-child the answer came.

"Yes. Yes, Joseph. I'm with you."

There are many questions about the Bible that we won't be able to answer until we get home. Many knotholes and snapshots. Many times we will muse, "I wonder . . ."

But in our wonderings, there are some questions we never need to ask. Does God care? Do we matter to God? Does he still love his children?

Through the small face of the stable-born baby, he says yes.

Yes, your sins are forgiven.

Yes, your name is written in heaven.

Yes, death has been defeated.

And yes, God has entered your world.

Immanuel. God is with us.

For Reflection and Discussion

1. Describe a time when you were caught between what God says and what seemed to make sense.

2. What is the connection between our obedience and divine guidance? Why is it pointless to ask God for direction for your life if you are disobeying some command of Scripture?

3. What instances in your past have caused you to question why God did what he did?

4. What generally happens to your attitude when you question God's handling of your life or circumstances? Is there a pattern you can discern?

5. Read Hebrews 3:12–19. What advice is given in verse 13 to help us obey God together? Note the close connection between obedience and belief in verses 18 and 19. What is this connection?

Chapter 2

MATTHEW

As Jesus was walking along, he saw a man named Matthew sitting at his tax collector's booth. "Follow me and be my disciple," Jesus said to him. So Matthew got up and followed him.

Later, Matthew invited Jesus and his disciples to his home as dinner guests, along with many tax collectors and other disreputable sinners. But when the Pharisees saw this, they asked his disciples, "Why does your teacher eat with such scum?"

When Jesus heard this, he said, "Healthy people don't need a doctor—sick people do." Then he added, "Now go and learn the meaning of this Scripture: 'I want you to show mercy, not offer sacrifices.' For I have come to call not those who think they are righteous, but those who know they are sinners."

{ MATT. 9:9–3 NLT }

FRIEND OF FLOPS

As Jesus was going down the road, he saw Matthew sitting at his tax-collection booth. 'Come, be my disciple,' Jesus said to him. So Matthew got up and followed him" (Matt. 9:9 NLT).

The surprise in this invitation is the one invited—a tax collector. Combine the greed of an embezzling executive with the presumption of a hokey television evangelist. Throw in the audacity of an ambulance-chasing lawyer and the cowardice of a drive-by sniper. Stir in a pinch of a pimp's morality, and finish it off with the drug peddler's code of ethics—and what do you have?

A first-century tax collector.

According to the Jews, these guys ranked barely above plankton on the food chain. Caesar permitted these Jewish citizens to tax almost anything—your boat, the fish you caught, your house, your crops. As long as Caesar got his due, they could keep the rest.

Matthew was a *public* tax collector. Private tax collectors hired other people to do the dirty work. Public publicans, like Matthew, just pulled their stretch limos into the poor side of town and set up shop. As crooked as corkscrews.

His given name was Levi, a priestly name (Mark 2:14; Luke 5:27–28). Did his parents aspire for him to enter the priesthood? If so, he was a flop in the family circle.

You can bet he was shunned. The neighborhood cookouts? Never invited. High-school reunions? Somehow his name was left off the list. The guy was avoided like streptococcus A. Everybody kept his distance from Matthew.

Everyone except Jesus. "'Come, be my disciple,' Jesus said to him. So Matthew got up and followed him" (Matt. 9:9 NLT).

Matthew must have been ripe. Jesus hardly had to tug. Within a punctuation mark, Matthew's shady friends and Jesus' green followers are swapping e-mail addresses. "Then Levi gave a big dinner for Jesus at his house. Many tax collectors and other people were eating there, too" (Luke 5:29).

What do you suppose led up to that party? Let's try to imagine. I can see Matthew going back to his office and packing up. He removes the Quisling of the Year Award from the wall and boxes up the Shady Business School certificate. His coworkers start asking questions.

"What's up, Matt? Headed on a cruise?"

"Hey, Matthew, the Missus kick you out?"

Matthew doesn't know what to say. He mumbles something about a job change. But as he reaches the door, he pauses. Holding his box full of office supplies, he looks back. They're giving him hangdog looks—kind of sad, puzzled.

He feels a lump in his throat. Oh, these guys aren't much. Parents warn their kids about this sort. Salty language. Mardi Gras morals. They keep the phone number of the bookie on speed dial. The bouncer at the Gentlemen's Club sends them birthday cards. But a friend is a friend. Yet what can he do? Invite them to meet Jesus? Yeah, right. They like preachers the way sheep like butchers. Tell them to tune in to the religious channel on TV? Then they'd think cotton-candy hair is a requirement for following Christ. What if he snuck little Torah tracts in their desks? Nah, they don't read.

So, not knowing what else to do, he shrugs his shoulders and gives them a nod. "These stupid allergies," he says, rubbing the mist from one eye.

Later that day the same thing happens. He goes to the bar to settle up his account. The décor is blue-collar chic: a seedy, smoky place with a Budweiser chandelier over the pool table and a jukebox in the corner. Not the country club, but for Matthew, it's his home on the way home.

And when he tells the owner he's moving on, the bartender responds, "Whoa, Matt. What's comin' down?"

Matthew mumbles an excuse about a transfer but leaves with an empty feeling in his gut.

Later on he meets up with Jesus at a diner and shares his problem. "It's my buddies—you know, the guys at the office. And the fellows at the bar."

"What about them?" Jesus asks.

"Well, we kinda run together, you know. I'm gonna miss 'em. Take Josh for instance—as slick as a can of Quaker State, but he visits orphans on Sunday. And Bruno at the gym? Can crunch you like a roach, but I've never had a better friend. He's posted bail for me three times."

Jesus motions for him to go on. "What's the problem?"

"Well, I'm gonna miss those guys. I mean, I've got nothing against Peter and James and John, Jesus . . . but they're Sunday morning, and I'm Saturday night. I've got my own circle, ya know?"

Jesus starts to smile and shake his head. "Matthew, Matthew, you think I came to quarantine you? Following me doesn't mean forgetting your friends. Just the opposite. I want to meet them."

"Are you serious?"

"Is the high priest a Jew?"

"But, Jesus, these guys . . . half of them are on parole. Josh hasn't worn socks since his bar mitzvah . . ."

"I'm not talking about a religious service, Matthew. Let me ask you— what do you like to do? Bowl? Play Monopoly? How's your golf game?"

Matthew's eyes brighten. "You ought to see me cook. I get on steaks like a whale on Jonah."

"Perfect." Jesus smiles. "Then throw a little going-away party. A hang-up-the-clipboard bash. Get the gang together."

Matthew's all over it. Calling the caterer, his housekeeper, his secretary. "Get the word out, Thelma. Drinks and dinner at my house tonight. Tell the guys to come and bring a date."

And so Jesus ends up at Matthew's house, a classy split-level with a view of the Sea of Galilee. Parked out front is everything from BMWs to Harleys to limos. And the crowd inside tells you this is anything but a clergy conference.

Earrings on the guys and tattoos on the girls. Moussified hair. Music that rumbles teeth roots. And buzzing around in the middle of the group is Matthew, making more connections than an electrician. He hooks up Peter with the tax collector bass club and Martha with the kitchen staff. Simon the Zealot meets a high-school debate partner. And Jesus? Beaming. What could be better? Sinners and saints in the same room, and no one's trying to determine who is which. But an hour or so into the evening the door opens, and an icy breeze blows in. "The Pharisees and the men who taught the law for the Pharisees began to complain to Jesus' followers, 'Why do you eat and drink with tax collectors and sinners?'" (Luke 5:30).

Enter the religious police and their thin-lipped piety. Big black books under arms. Cheerful as Siberian prison guards. Clerical collars so tight that veins bulge. They like to grill too. But not steaks.

Matthew is the first to feel the heat. "Some religious fellow you are," one says, practically pulling an eyebrow muscle. "Look at the people you hang out with."

Matthew doesn't know whether to get mad or get out. Before he has time to choose, Jesus intervenes, explaining that Matthew is right where he needs to be. "Healthy people don't need a doctor—sick people do. I have come to call not those who think they are righteous, but those who know they are sinners and need to repent" (vv. 31–32 NLT).

Quite a story. Matthew goes from double-dealer to disciple. He throws a party that makes the religious right uptight, but Christ proud. The good guys look good, and the bad guys hit the road. Some story indeed.

What do we do with it?

That depends on which side of the tax collector's table you find yourself. You and I are Matthew. Don't look at me that way. There's enough hustler in the best of us to qualify for Matthew's table. Maybe you've never taken taxes, but you've taken liberty with the truth, taken credit that wasn't yours, taken advantage of the weak. You and me? Matthew.

If you're still at the table, you receive an invitation. "Follow me." So what if you've got a rube reputation? So did Matthew. You may end up writing your own gospel.

If you've left the table, you receive a clarification. You don't have to be weird to follow Jesus. You don't have to stop liking your friends to follow him. Just the opposite. A few introductions would be nice. Do you know how to grill a steak?

Sometime ago I was asked to play a game of golf. The foursome included two preachers, a church leader, and a "Matthew, B.C." The thought of four hours with three Christians, two of whom were pulpiteers, did not appeal to him. His best friend, a Christ follower and his boss, insisted, so he agreed. I'm happy to report that he proclaimed the experience painless. On the ninth hole he turned to one of us and said, smiling, "I'm so glad you guys are normal." I think he meant this: "I'm glad you didn't get in my face or club me with a King James driver. Thanks for laughing at my jokes and telling a few yourself. Thanks for being normal." We didn't lower standards. But neither did we saddle a high horse. We were nice. Normal and nice.

Discipleship is sometimes defined by being normal.

A woman in a small Arkansas community was a single mom with a frail baby. Her neighbor would stop by every few days and keep the child so she could shop. After some weeks her neighbor shared more than time; she shared her faith, and the woman did what Matthew did. She followed Christ.

The friends of the young mother objected. "Do you know what those people teach?" they contested.

"Here is what I know," she told them. "They held my baby."[1]

I think Jesus likes that kind of answer, don't you?

FOR REFLECTION AND DISCUSSION

1. What's good about having saints and sinners in the same room?
2. What's good about not trying to figure out who belongs to which group?
3. Why did Matthew's party make the religious right uptight?
4. What parallel situations do you see today? Do you generally respond to them like Christ or like the religious leaders? Why?
5. What does Max really mean when he asks, "Do you know how to grill a steak?" How would you answer his question?

⨯⨯

Chapter 3

WOMAN WHO WASHED JESUS' FEET

One of the Pharisees asked Jesus to have dinner with him, so Jesus went to his home and sat down to eat. When a certain immoral woman from that city heard he was eating there, she brought a beautiful alabaster jar filled with expensive perfume. Then she knelt behind him at his feet, weeping. Her tears fell on his feet, and she wiped them off with her hair. Then she kept kissing his feet and putting perfume on them.

When the Pharisee who had invited him saw this, he said to himself, "If this man were a prophet, he would know what kind of woman is touching him. She's a sinner!" . . .

[Jesus said,] "I tell you, her sins—and they are many—have been forgiven, so she has shown me much love. But a person who is forgiven little shows only little love."

{ LUKE 7:36–39, 47 NLT }

The 7:47 Principle

Could two people be more different?

He is looked up to. She is looked down on.

He is a church leader. She is a streetwalker.

He makes a living promoting standards. She's made a living breaking them.

He's hosting the party. She's crashing it.

Ask the other residents of Capernaum to point out the more pious of the two, and they'll pick Simon. Why, after all, he's a student of theology, a man of the cloth. Anyone would pick him. Anyone, that is, except Jesus. Jesus knew them both. And Jesus would pick the woman. Jesus does pick the woman. And, what's more, he tells Simon why.

Not that Simon wants to know. His mind is elsewhere. *How did this whore get in my house?* He doesn't know whom to yell at first, the woman or the servant who let her in. After all, this dinner is a formal affair. Invitation only. Upper crust. Crème de la crème. Who let the riffraff in?

Simon is angry. *Just look at her—groveling at Jesus' feet. Kissing them, no less! Why, if Jesus were who he says he is, he would have nothing to do with this woman.*

One of the lessons Simon learned that day was this: Don't think thoughts you don't want Jesus to hear. For Jesus heard them, and when he did, he chose to share a few of his own.

"Simon," he said to the Pharisee, "I have something to say to you."

"All right, Teacher," Simon replied, "go ahead."

Then Jesus told him this story: "A man loaned money to two people—five hundred pieces of silver to one and fifty pieces to the other. But neither of them could repay him, so he kindly forgave them both, canceling their debts. Who do you suppose loved him more after that?"

Simon answered, "I suppose the one for whom he canceled the larger debt."

"That's right," Jesus said. Then he turned to the woman and said to Simon, "Look at this woman kneeling here. When I entered your home, you didn't offer me water to wash the dust from my feet, but she has washed them with her tears and wiped them with her hair. You didn't greet me with a kiss, but from the time I first came in, she has not stopped kissing my feet. You neglected the courtesy of olive oil to anoint my head, but she has anointed my feet with rare perfume. I tell you, her sins—and they are many—have been forgiven, so she has shown me much love. But a person who is forgiven little shows only little love." (Luke 7:40–47 NLT)

Simon invites Jesus to his house but treats him like an unwanted step-uncle. No customary courtesies. No kiss of greeting. No washing his feet. No oil for his head.

Or, in modern terms, no one opened the door for him, took his coat, or shook his hand. Count Dracula has better manners.

Simon does nothing to make Jesus feel welcome. The woman, however, does everything that Simon didn't. We aren't told her name. Just her reputation—a sinner. A prostitute most likely. She has no invitation to the party and no standing in the community. (Imagine a hooker in a tight dress showing up at the parsonage during the pastor's Christmas party. Heads turn. Faces blush. Gasp!)

But people's opinions didn't stop her from coming. It's not for them she has come. It's for him. Her every move is measured and meaningful. Each gesture extravagant. She puts her cheek to his feet, still dusty from the path. She has no water, but she has tears. She has no towel, but she has her hair. She uses both to bathe the feet of Christ. As one translation reads, "she rained tears" on his feet (v. 44 MSG). She opens a vial of perfume, perhaps her only possession of worth, and massages it into his skin. The aroma is as inescapable as the irony.

You'd think Simon of all people would show such love. Is he not the reverend of the church, the student of Scripture? But he is harsh, distant. You'd think the woman would avoid Jesus. Is she not the woman of the night, the town hussy? But she can't resist him. Simon's "love" is calibrated and stingy. Her love, on the other hand, is extravagant and risky.

How do we explain the difference between the two? Training? Education? Money? No, for Simon has outdistanced her in all three.

But there is one area in which the woman leaves him eating dust. Think about it. What one discovery has she made that Simon hasn't? What one treasure does she cherish that Simon doesn't? Simple. God's love. We don't know when she received it. We aren't told how she heard about it. Did she overhear Jesus' words "Your Father is merciful" (Luke 6:36 ESV)? Was she nearby when Jesus had compassion on the widow of Nain? Did someone tell her how Jesus touched lepers and turned tax collectors into disciples? We don't know. But we know this. She came thirsty. Thirsty from guilt. Thirsty from regret. Thirsty from countless nights of making love and finding none. She came thirsty.

And when Jesus hands her the goblet of grace, she drinks. She doesn't just taste or nip. She doesn't dip her finger and lick it or take the cup and sip it. She lifts the liquid to her lips and drinks, gulping and swallowing like the parched pilgrim she is. She drinks until the mercy flows down her chin and onto her neck and chest. She drinks until every inch of her soul is moist and soft. She comes thirsty and she drinks. She drinks deeply.

Simon, on the other hand, doesn't even know he is thirsty. People like Simon don't need grace; they analyze it. They don't request mercy; they debate and prorate it. It wasn't that Simon couldn't be forgiven; he just never asks to be.

So while she drinks up, he puffs up. While she has ample love to give, he has no love to offer. Why? The 7:47 Principle. Read again verse 47 of chapter 7: "A person who is forgiven little shows only little love." Just like the jumbo jet, the 7:47 Principle has wide wings. Just like the aircraft, this truth can lift you to another level. Read it one more time. "A person who is forgiven little shows only little love." In other words, we can't give what we've never received. If we've never received love, how can we love others?

But, oh, how we try! As if we can conjure up love by the sheer force of will. As if there is within us a distillery of affection that lacks only a piece of wood or a hotter fire. We poke it and stoke it with resolve. What's our typical strategy for treating a troubled relationship? Try harder.

"My spouse needs my forgiveness? I don't know how, but I'm going to give it."

"I don't care how much it hurts, I'm going to be nice to that bum."

"I'm supposed to love my neighbor? Okay. By golly, I will."

So we try. Teeth clinched. Jaw firm. We're going to love if it kills us! And it may do just that.

Could it be we are missing a step? Could it be that the first step of love is not toward them but toward him? Could it be that the secret to loving is receiving? You give love by first receiving it. "We love, because He first loved us" (1 John 4:19 NASB).

Long to be more loving? Begin by accepting your place as a dearly loved child. "Be imitators of God, therefore, as dearly loved children and live a life of love, just as Christ loved us" (Eph. 5:1–2 NIV).

Want to learn to forgive? Then consider how you've been forgiven. "Be kind and compassionate to one another, forgiving each other, just as in Christ God forgave you" (Eph. 4:32 NIV).

Finding it hard to put others first? Think of the way Christ put you first. "Though he was God, he did not think of equality with God as something to cling to" (Phil. 2:6 NLT).

Need more patience? Drink from the patience of God (2 Pet. 3:9). Is generosity an elusive virtue? Then consider how generous God has been with you (Rom. 5:8). Having trouble putting up with ungrateful relatives or cranky neighbors? God puts up with you when you act the same. "He is kind to the ungrateful and wicked" (Luke 6:35 NIV).

Can't we love like this?

Not without God's help we can't. Oh, we may succeed for a time. We, like Simon, may open a door. But our relationships need more than a social gesture. Some of our spouses need a foot washing. A few of our friends need a flood of tears. Our children need to be covered in the oil of our love.

But if we haven't received these things ourselves, how can we give them to others? Apart from God, "the heart is deceitful above all things" (Jer. 17:9 NIV). A marriage-saving love is not within us. A friendship-preserving devotion cannot be found in our hearts. We need help from an outside source. A transfusion. Would we love as God loves? Then we start by receiving God's love.

We preachers have been guilty of skipping the first step. "Love each other!" we tell our churches. "Be patient, kind, forgiving," we urge. But instructing people to love without telling them they are loved is like telling them to write a check without our making a deposit in their accounts. No wonder so many relationships are overdrawn. Hearts have insufficient love. The apostle John models the right sequence. He makes a deposit before he tells us to write the check. First, the deposit:

> God showed how much he loved us by sending his one and only Son into the world so that we might have eternal life through him. This is real love—not that we loved God, but that he loved us and sent his Son as a sacrifice to take away our sins. (1 John 4:9–10 NLT)

And then, having made such an outrageous, eye-opening deposit, John calls on you and me to pull out the checkbook: "Dear friends, since God loved us that much, we surely ought to love each other" (v. 11 NLT).

The secret to loving is living loved. This is the forgotten first step in relationships. Remember Paul's prayer? "Your roots will grow down into God's love and keep you strong" (Eph. 3:17 NLT). As a tree draws nutrients from the soil, we draw nourishment from the Father. But what if the tree has no contact with the soil?

I was thinking of this yesterday as I disassembled our Christmas tree. That's my traditional New Year's Day chore. Remove the ornaments, carry out the tree, and sweep up all the needles. There are thousands of them! The tree is falling apart. Blame it on bad rooting. For two weeks this tree has been planted in a metal bowl. What comes from a tree holder?

Old Simon had the same problem. Impressive to look at, nicely decorated, but he falls apart when you give him a shove or two.

Sound familiar? Does bumping into certain people leave you brittle, breakable, and fruitless? Do you easily fall apart? If so, your love may be grounded in the wrong soil. It may be rooted in their love (which is fickle) or in your resolve to love (which is frail). John urges us to "rely on the love God has for us" (1 John 4:16 NIV, emphasis mine). He alone is the power source.

Many people tell us to love. Only God gives us the power to do so.

We know what God wants us to do. "This is what God commands: . . . that we love each other" (1 John 3:23). But how can we? How can we be kind to the vow breakers? To those who are unkind to us? How can we be patient with people who have the warmth of a vulture and the tenderness of a porcupine? How can we forgive the moneygrubbers and backstabbers we meet, love, and marry? How can we love as God loves? We want to. We long to. But how can we?

By living loved. By following the 7:47 Principle: Receive first, love second.

Want to give it a try? Let's carry this principle up the Mount Everest of love writings. More than one person has hailed 1 Corinthians 13 as the finest chapter in the Bible. No words get to the heart of loving people like these verses. And no verses get to the heart of the chapter like verses 4 through 8.

Love is patient, love is kind. It does not envy, it does not boast, it is not proud. It is not rude, it is not self-seeking, it is not easily angered, it keeps no record of wrongs. Love does not delight in evil but rejoices with the truth. It always protects, always trusts, always hopes, always perseveres. Love never fails. (NIV)

Several years ago someone challenged me to replace the word *love* in this passage with my name. I did and became a liar. "Max is patient, Max is kind. Max does not envy, he does not boast, he is not proud. . . ." That's enough! Stop right there! Those words are false. Max is not patient. Max is not kind. Ask my wife and kids. Max can be an out-and-out clod! That's my problem.

And for years that was my problem with this paragraph. It set a standard I could not meet. No one can meet it. No one, that is, except Christ. Does this passage not describe the measureless love of God? Let's insert Christ's name in place of the word *love,* and see if it rings true.

Jesus is patient, Jesus is kind. Jesus does not envy, he does not boast, he is not proud. Jesus is not rude, he is not self-seeking, he is not easily angered, he keeps no record of wrongs. Jesus does not delight in evil but rejoices with the truth. Jesus always protects, always trusts, always hopes, always perseveres. Jesus never fails.

Rather than let this scripture remind us of a love we cannot produce, let it remind us of a love we cannot resist—God's love.

Some of you are so thirsty for this type of love. Those who should have loved you didn't. Those who could have loved you didn't. You were left at the hospital. Left at the altar. Left with an empty bed. Left with a broken heart. Left with your question "Does anybody love me?"

Please listen to heaven's answer. God loves you. Personally. Powerfully. Passionately. Others have promised and failed. But God has promised and succeeded. He loves you with an unfailing love. And his love—if you will let it—can fill you and leave you with a love worth giving.

So come. Come thirsty and drink deeply.

FOR REFLECTION AND DISCUSSION

1. Read 1 John 4:19. Do you agree that we can't give what we haven't received? Explain.

2. How does someone "receive" love? How does someone "refuse" love?

3. How can you cover others "in the oil" of your love? How do you need to be covered "in the oil" of others' love?

4. Read Luke 7:36–50. What principle did Jesus develop in verse 47? How does this principle relate to you? Explain.

5. Think of the person closest to you (whether spouse, friend, child, parent, etc.). Make a list by responding to the question "How can I do a better job of showing love to this person?" Before the end of the week, begin doing at least one of the things you wrote on the list.

Chapter 4

MEPHIBOSHETH

(Saul's son Jonathan had a son named Mephibosheth, who was crippled in both feet. He was five years old when the news came from Jezreel that Saul and Jonathan were dead. Mephibosheth's nurse had picked him up and run away. But as she hurried to leave, she dropped him, and now he was lame. . . .)

The king asked, "Is anyone left in Saul's family? I want to show God's kindness to that person."

Ziba answered the king, "Jonathan has a son still living who is crippled in both feet."

The king asked Ziba, "Where is this son?"

Ziba answered, "He is at the house of Makir son of Ammiel in Lo Debar."

Then King David had servants bring Jonathan's son from the house of Makir son of Ammiel in Lo Debar. Mephibosheth, Jonathan's son, came before David and bowed facedown on the floor.

David said, "Mephibosheth!"

Mephibosheth said, "I am your servant."

David said to him, "Don't be afraid. I will be kind to you for your father Jonathan's sake. I will give you back all the land of your grandfather Saul, and you will always eat at my table."

Mephibosheth bowed to David again and said, "You are being very kind to me, your servant! And I am no better than a dead dog!"

Then King David called Saul's servant Ziba. David said to him, "I have given your master's grandson everything that belonged to Saul and his family. You, your sons, and your servants will farm the land and harvest the crops. Then your family will have food to eat. But Mephibosheth, your master's grandson, will always eat at my table."

(Now Ziba had fifteen sons and twenty servants.) Ziba said to King David, "I, your servant, will do everything my master, the king, commands me."

So Mephibosheth ate at David's table as if he were one of the king's sons.

{ 2 SAM. 4:4; 9:3–11 }

The Privilege of Paupers

Warning: *The content of this chapter is likely to cause hunger. You might want to read it in the kitchen.*

My first ministry position was in Miami, Florida. In our congregation we had more than our share of southern ladies who loved to cook. I fit in well because I was a single guy who loved to eat. The church was fond of having Sunday evening potluck dinners, and about once a quarter they *feasted.*

Some church dinners live up to the "potluck" name. The cooks empty the pot, and you try your luck. Not so with this church. Our potlucks were major events. Area grocery stores asked us to advise them in advance so they could stock their shelves. Cookbook sales went up. People never before seen in the pews could be found in the food line. For the women it was an unofficial cookoff, and for the men it was an unabashed pigout.

My, it was good, a veritable cornucopia of Corningware. Juicy ham bathed in pineapple, baked beans, pickled relish, pecan pie . . . (Oops, I just drooled on my computer keyboard.) Ever wondered why there are so many hefty preachers? You enter the ministry for meals like those.

As a bachelor I counted on potluck dinners for my survival strategy. While others were planning what to cook, I was studying the storage techniques of camels. Knowing I should bring something, I'd make it a point to raid my kitchen shelves on Sunday afternoon. The result was pitiful: One time I took a half-empty jar of Planters peanuts; another time I made a half-dozen jelly sandwiches. One of my better offerings was an unopened sack of chips; a more meager gift was a can of tomato soup, also unopened.

Wasn't much, but no one ever complained. In fact, the way those ladies acted, you would've thought I brought the Thanksgiving turkey. They'd take my jar of peanuts and set it on the long table with the rest of the food and hand me a plate. "Go ahead, Max, don't be bashful. Fill up your plate." And I would! Mashed potatoes and gravy. Roast beef. Fried chicken. I took a little bit of everything, except the peanuts.

I came like a pauper and ate like a king!

Though Paul never attended a potluck, he would have loved the symbolism. He would say that Christ does for us precisely what those women did for me. He welcomes us to his table by virtue of his love and our request. It is not our offerings that grant us a place at the feast; indeed, anything we bring appears puny at his table. Our admission of hunger is the only demand, for "Blessed are those who hunger and thirst for righteousness, for they shall be filled" (Matt. 5:6 NKJV).

Our hunger, then, is not a yearning to be avoided but rather a God-given desire to be heeded. Our weakness is not to be dismissed but to be confessed. Isn't this at the heart of Paul's words when he writes, "When we were unable to help ourselves, at the right time, Christ died for us, although we were living against God. Very few people will die to save the life of someone else. Although perhaps for a good person someone might possibly die. But God shows his great love for us in this way: Christ died for us while we were still sinners" (Rom. 5:6–8).

THE PORTRAIT OF A PAUPER

Paul's portrait of us is not attractive. We were "unable to help ourselves," "living against God," "sinners," and "God's enemies" (Rom. 5:6, 8, 10). Such are the people for whom God died.

Family therapist Paul Faulkner tells of the man who set out to adopt a troubled teenage girl. One would question the father's logic. The girl was destructive, disobedient, and dishonest. One day she came home from school and ransacked the house looking for money. By the time he arrived, she was gone and the house was in shambles.

Upon hearing of her actions, friends urged him not to finalize the adoption. "Let her go," they said. "After all, she's not really your daughter." His response was simply. "Yes, I know. But I told her she was."[1]

God, too, has made a covenant to adopt his people. His covenant is not invalidated by our rebellion. It's one thing to love us when we are strong, obedient, and willing. But when we ransack his house and steal what is his? This is the test of love.

And God passes the test. "God shows his great love for us in this way: Christ died for us while we were still sinners" (5:8).

The ladies at our church didn't see me and my peanuts and say, "Come back when you've learned to cook."

The father didn't look at the wrecked house and say, "Come back when you've learned respect."

God didn't look at our frazzled lives and say, "I'll die for you when you deserve it."

Nor did David look at Mephibosheth and say, "I'll rescue you when you've learned to walk."

Mephibo-*what*?

Mephibosheth. When you hear his story you'll see why I mention his name. Blow the dust off the books of 1 and 2 Samuel, and there you'll see him.

(Saul's son Jonathan had a son named Mephibosheth, who was crippled in both feet. He was five years old when the news came from Jezreel that Saul and Jonathan were dead. Mephibosheth's nurse had picked him up and run away. But as she hurried to leave, she dropped him, and now he was lame.) (2 Sam. 4:4)

The parentheses around the verse are not typos. Mephibosheth is bracketed into the Bible. The verse doesn't tell us much, just his name (Mephibosheth), his calamity (dropped by his nurse), his deformity (crippled), and then it moves on.

But that's enough to raise a few questions. Who was this boy? Why is this story in Scripture? A bit of background would be helpful.

Mephibosheth was the son of Jonathan, the grandson of Saul, who was the first king of Israel. Saul and Jonathan were killed in battle, leaving the throne to be occupied by David. In those days the new king often staked out his territory by exterminating the family of the previous king.

David had no intention of following this tradition, but the family of Saul didn't know that. So they hurried to escape. Of special concern to them was five-year-old Mephibosheth, for upon the deaths of his father and uncle, he was the presumptive heir to the throne. If David was intent on murdering Saul's heirs, this boy would be first on his list. So the family got out of Dodge. But in the haste of the moment, Mephibosheth slipped from the arms of his nurse, permanently damaging both feet. For the rest of his life he would be a cripple.

If his story is beginning to sound familiar, it should. You and he have a lot in common. Weren't you also born of royalty? And don't you carry the wounds of a fall? And hasn't each of us lived in fear of a king we have never seen?

Mephibosheth would understand Paul's portrait of us paupers, "when we were unable to help ourselves . . ." (Rom. 5:6). For nearly two decades the young prince lived in a distant land, unable to walk to the king, too fearful to talk to the king. He was unable to help himself.

Meanwhile, David's kingdom flourished. Under his leadership, Israel grew to ten times its original size. He knew no defeat on the battlefield nor insurrection in his court. Israel was at peace. The people were thankful. And David, the shepherd made king, did not forget his promise to Jonathan.

THE PROMISE OF A KING

David and Jonathan were like two keys on a piano keyboard. Alone they made music, but together they made harmony. Jonathan "loved David as much as he loved himself" (1 Sam. 20:17). Their legendary friendship met its ultimate test the day David learned that Saul was trying to kill him. Jonathan pledged to save David and asked his friend one favor in return: "You must never stop showing your kindness to my family, even when the LORD has destroyed all your enemies from the earth. So Jonathan made an agreement with David" (1 Sam. 20:15–16).

Don't you know this was a tender memory for David? Can't you imagine him reflecting on this moment years later? Standing on the balcony overlooking the safe city. Astride his steed riding through the abundant fields. Dressed in armor inspecting his capable army. Were there times when he was overwhelmed with gratitude? Were there times when he thought, *Had it not been for Jonathan saving my life, none of this would have happened?*

Perhaps such a moment of reflection prompted him to turn to his servants and ask, "Is anyone still left in Saul's family? I want to show kindness to that person for Jonathan's sake!" (2 Sam. 9:1).

Those who are prone to extend grace tend to ask such questions. Can't I do something for somebody? Can't I be kind to someone because others have been kind to me? This isn't a political maneuver. David isn't seeking to do good to be applauded by people. Nor is he doing something good so someone will do something for him. He is driven by the singular thought that he, too, was once weak. And in his weakness he was helped. David, while hiding from Saul, qualified for Paul's epitaph, "when we were unable to help ourselves" (Rom. 5:6).

David was delivered; now he desires to do the same. A servant named Ziba knows of a descendant. "'Jonathan has a son still living who is crippled in both feet.' The king asked Ziba, 'Where is this son?' Ziba answered, 'He is at the house of Makir son of Ammiel in Lo Debar'" (2 Sam. 9:3–4).

Just one sentence and David knew he had more than he bargained for. The boy was "crippled in both feet." Who would have blamed David for asking Ziba, "Are there any other options? Any healthy family members?"

Who would have faulted him for reasoning, *A cripple would not fit well into the castle crowd. Only the elite walk these floors; this kid can't even walk! And what service could he provide? No wealth, no education, no training. And who knows what he looks like? All these years he's been living in . . . what was it again? Lo Debar? Even the name means "barren place." Surely there is someone I can help who isn't so needy.*

But such words were never spoken. David's only response was, "Where is this son?" (v. 4).

This son. One wonders how long it had been since Mephibosheth was referred to as a son. In all previous references he was called a cripple. Every mention of him thus far is followed by his handicap. But the words of David make no mention of his affliction. He doesn't ask, "Where is Mephibosheth, this problem child?" but rather asks, "Where is this son?"

Many of you know what it's like to carry a stigma. Each time your name is mentioned, your calamity follows.

"Have you heard from John lately? You know, the fellow who got divorced?"

"We got a letter from Jerry. Remember him, the alcoholic?"

"Sharon is in town. What a shame that she has to raise those kids alone."

"I saw Melissa today. I don't know why she can't keep a job."

Like a pesky sibling, your past follows you wherever you go. Isn't there anyone who sees you for who you are and not what you did? Yes. There is One who does. Your King. When God speaks of you, he doesn't mention your plight, pain, or problem; he lets you share his glory. He calls you his child.

> He will not always accuse us,
>> and he will not be angry forever.
> He has not punished us as our sins should be punished;
>> he has not repaid us for the evil we have done.
> As high as the sky is above the earth,

so great is his love for those who respect him.
He has taken our sins away from us
as far as the east is from the west.
The Lord has mercy on those who respect him,
as a father has mercy on his children.
He knows how we were made;
he remembers that we are dust. (Ps. 103:9–14)

Mephibosheth carried his stigma for twenty years. When people mentioned his name, they mentioned his problem. But when the king mentioned his name, he called him "son." And one word from the palace offsets a thousand voices in the streets.

David's couriers journeyed to Mephibosheth's door, carried him to a chariot, and escorted him to the palace. He was taken before the king, where he bowed facedown on the floor and confessed, "I am your servant" (2 Sam. 9:6). His fear is understandable. Though he may have been told that David was kind, what assurance did he have? Though the emissaries surely told him that David meant no harm, he was afraid. (Wouldn't you be?) The anxiety was on the face that faced the floor. David's first words to him were, "Don't be afraid."

By the way, your king has been known to say the same. Are you aware that the most repeated command from the lips of Jesus was, "Fear not"? Are you aware that the command from heaven not to be afraid appears in every book of the Bible?

Mephibosheth had been called, found, and rescued, but he still needed assurance. Don't we all? Don't we, like the trembling guest, need assurance that we are bowing before a gracious king? Paul says we have that assurance. The apostle points to the cross as our guarantee of God's love. "God shows his great love for us in this way: Christ died for us while we were still sinners" (Rom. 5:8). God proved his love for us by sacrificing his Son.

Formerly God had sent prophets to preach: Now he has sent his son to die. Earlier God commissioned angels to aid, now he has offered his son to redeem. When we tremble he points us to the splattered blood on the splintered beams and says, "Don't be afraid."

During the early days of the Civil War a Union soldier was arrested on charges of desertion. Unable to prove his innocence, he was condemned and sentenced to die a deserter's death. His appeal found its way to the desk of Abraham Lincoln. The president felt mercy for the soldier and signed a pardon. The soldier returned to service, fought the entirety of the war, and was killed in the last battle. Found within his breast pocket was the signed letter of the president.[2]

Close to the heart of the soldier were his leader's words of pardon. He found courage in grace. I wonder how many thousands more have found courage in the emblazoned cross of their king.

THE PRIVILEGE OF ADOPTION

Just as David kept his promise to Jonathan, so God keeps his promise to us. The name Mephibosheth means "he who scatters shame." And that is exactly what David intended to do for the young prince.

In swift succession David returned to Mephibosheth all his land, crops, and servants and then insisted that the cripple eat at the king's table. Not just once but four times!

> "I will give you back all the land of your grandfather Saul, and *you will always eat at my table.*"
>
> "Mephibosheth . . . *will always eat at my table.*"
>
> "So *Mephibosheth ate at David's table* as if he were one of the king's sons."
>
> "Mephibosheth lived in Jerusalem, because *he always ate at the king's table. And he was crippled in both feet.*" (2 Sam. 9:7, 10, 11, 13, italics mine)

Pause and envision the scene in the royal dining room. May I turn my pen over to Charles Swindoll to assist you?

The dinner bell rings through the king's palace and David comes to the head of the table and sits down. In a few moments Amnon—clever, crafty, Amnon—sits to the left of David. Lovely and gracious Tamar, a charming and beautiful young woman, arrives and sits beside Amnon. And then across the way, Solomon walks slowly from his study; precocious, brilliant, preoccupied Solomon. The heir apparent slowly sits down. And then Absalom—handsome, winsome Absalom with beautiful flowing hair, black as a raven, down to his shoulders—sits down. That particular evening Joab, the courageous warrior and David's commander of the troops, has been invited to dinner. Muscular, bronzed Joab is seated near the king. Afterward they wait. They hear the shuffling of feet, the clump, clump, clump of the crutches as Mephibosheth rather awkwardly finds his place at the table and slips into his seat . . . and the tablecloth covers his feet. I ask you: Did Mephibosheth understand grace?[3]

And I ask you, do you see our story in his?

Children of royalty, crippled by the fall, permanently marred by sin. Living parenthetical lives in the chronicles of earth only to be remembered by the king. Driven not by our beauty but by his promise, he calls us to himself and invites us to take a permanent place at his table. Though we often limp more than we walk, we take our place next to the other sinners-made-saints and we share in God's glory.

May I share a partial list of what awaits you at his table?

You are beyond condemnation (Rom. 8:1).
You are delivered from the law (Rom. 7:6).
You are near God (Eph. 2:13).
You are delivered from the power of evil (Col. 1:13).
You are a member of his kingdom (Col. 1:13).
You are justified (Rom. 5:1).
You are perfect (Heb. 10:14).

You have been adopted (Rom. 8:15).

You have access to God at any moment (Eph. 2:18).

You are a part of his priesthood (1 Pet. 2:5).

You will never be abandoned (Heb. 13:5).

You have an imperishable inheritance (1 Pet. 1:4).

You are a partner with Christ in life (Col. 3:4) and privilege
(Eph. 2:6), suffering (2 Tim. 2:12), and service (1 Cor. 1:9).

You are a:

> member of his body (1 Cor. 12:13),
>
> branch in the vine (John 15:5),
>
> stone in the building (Eph 2:19–22),
>
> bride for the groom (Eph. 5:25–27),
>
> priest in the new generation (1 Pet. 2:9), and a
>
> dwelling place of the Spirit (1 Cor. 6:19).

You possess (get this!) every spiritual blessing possible. "In Christ, God has given us every spiritual blessing in the heavenly world" (Eph. 1:3). This is the gift offered to the lowliest sinner on earth. Who could make such an offer but God? "From him we all received one gift after another" (John 1:16).

Paul speaks for us all when he asks,

Have you ever come on anything quite like this extravagant love of God, this deep, deep, wisdom? It's way over our heads. We'll never figure it out.

> "Is there anyone around who can explain God?
> Anyone smart enough to tell him what to do?
> Anyone who has done him such a huge favor
> that God has to ask his advice?"
> Everything comes from him;
> Everything comes through him;

Everything ends up in him.

Always glory! Always praise!

Yes. Yes. Yes. (Rom. 11:33–36 MSG)

Like Mephibosheth, we are sons of the King. And like me in Miami, our greatest offering is peanuts compared to what we are given.

FOR REFLECTION AND DISCUSSION

1. "It is not our offerings that grant us a place at the feast; indeed, anything we bring appears puny at his table. Our admission of hunger is the only demand." What does Max mean by admitting our "hunger"? How do we do this? Have you done this? Explain.

2. "God didn't look at our frazzled lives and say, 'I'll die for you when you deserve it.'" Had God said such a thing, how would that affect you right now? Has anyone ever deserved for God to die for them? Explain.

3. Consider the list of blessings at God's table found on pages 39–40 in this chapter. Which of these is most precious to you? Why? Which of these blessings seems most distant to you? Why? How can knowledge of these blessings practically affect the way you live?

4. Read Matthew 5:6. What group of people does Jesus describe in this verse? What promise does he give to them?

5. Do you believe you are included in this group? Explain.

❧

Chapter 5

SAMARITAN WOMAN

Jesus, tired from the long walk, sat wearily beside the well about noontime. Soon a Samaritan woman came to draw water, and Jesus said to her, "Please give me a drink."

The woman was surprised, for Jews refuse to have anything to do with Samaritans. She said to Jesus, "You are a Jew, and I am a Samaritan woman. Why are you asking me for a drink?"

Jesus replied, "If you only knew the gift God has for you and who you are speaking to, you would ask me, and I would give you living water."

"But sir, you don't have a rope or a bucket," she said, "and this well is very deep. Where would you get this living water? And besides, do you think you're greater than our ancestor Jacob, who gave us this well? How can you offer better water than he and his sons and his animals enjoyed?"

Jesus replied, "Anyone who drinks this water will soon become thirsty again. But those who drink the water I give will never be thirsty again. It becomes a fresh, bubbling spring within them, giving them eternal life."

"Please, sir," the woman said, "give me this water! Then I'll never be thirsty again, and I won't have to come here to get water."

"Go and get your husband," Jesus told her.

"I don't have a husband," the woman replied.

Jesus said, "You're right! You don't have a husband—for you have had five husbands, and you aren't even married to the man you're living with now. You certainly spoke the truth!"

"Sir," the woman said, "you must be a prophet.". . .

"I know the Messiah is coming—the one who is called Christ. When he comes, he will explain everything to us."

Then Jesus told her, "I AM the Messiah!" . . .

The woman left her water jar beside the well and ran back to the village, telling everyone, "Come and see a man who told me everything I ever did! Could he possibly be the Messiah?"

{ JOHN 4:6–7, 9–19, 25–26, 28–29 NLT }

TWO TOMBSTONES

I had driven by the place countless times. Daily I passed the small plot of land on the way to my office. Daily I told myself, *Someday I need to stop there.*

Today, that "someday" came. I convinced a tight-fisted schedule to give me thirty minutes, and I drove in.

The intersection appears no different from any other in San Antonio: a Burger King, a Rodeway Inn, a restaurant. But turn northwest, go under the cast-iron sign, and you will find yourself on an island of history that is holding its own against the river of progress.

The name on the sign? Locke Hill Cemetery.

As I parked, a darkened sky threatened rain. A lonely path invited me to walk through the two-hundred-plus tombstones. The fatherly oak trees arched above me, providing a ceiling for the solemn chambers. Tall grass, still wet from the morning dew, brushed my ankles.

The tombstones, though weathered and chipped, were alive with yesterday.

Ruhet in herrn accents the markers that bear names like Schmidt, Faustman, Grundmeyer, and Eckert.

Ruth Lacey is buried there. Born in the days of Napoleon—1807. Died over a century ago—1877.

I stood on the same spot where a mother wept on a cold day some eight decades past. The tombstone read simply, "Baby Boldt—Born and died December 10, 1910."

Eighteen-year-old Harry Ferguson was laid to rest in 1883 under these words, "Sleep sweetly tired young pilgrim." I wondered what wearied him so.

Then I saw it. It was chiseled into a tombstone on the northern end of the cemetery. The stone marks the destination of the body of Grace Llewellen Smith. No date of birth is listed, no date of death. Just the names of her two husbands, and this epitaph:

Sleeps, but rests not.
Loved, but was loved not.
Tried to please, but pleased not.
Died as she lived—alone.

Words of futility.

I stared at the marker and wondered about Grace Llewellen Smith. I wondered about her life. I wondered if she'd written the words . . . or just lived them. I wondered if she deserved the pain. I wondered if she was bitter or beaten. I wondered if she was plain. I wondered if she was beautiful. I wondered why some lives are so fruitful while others are so futile.

I caught myself wondering aloud, "Mrs. Smith, what broke your heart?"

Raindrops smudged my ink as I copied the words.

Loved, but was loved not . . .

Long nights. Empty beds. Silence. No response to messages left. No return to letters written. No love exchanged for love given.

Tried to please, but pleased not . . .

I could hear the hatchet of disappointment.

"How many times do I have to tell you?" Chop.

"You'll never amount to anything." Chop. Chop.

"Why can't you do anything right?" Chop, chop, chop.

Died as she lived—alone.

How many Grace Llewellen Smiths are there? How many people will die in the loneliness in which they are living? The homeless in Atlanta. The happy-hour hopper in LA. A bag lady in Miami. The preacher in Nashville. Any person who doubts whether the world needs him. Any person who is convinced that no one really cares.

Any person who has been given a ring, but never a heart; criticism, but never a chance; a bed, but never rest.

These are the victims of futility.

And unless someone intervenes, unless something happens, the epitaph of Grace Smith will be theirs.

That's why the story you are about to read is significant. It's the story of another tombstone. This time, however, the tombstone doesn't mark the death of a person—it marks the birth. Her eyes squint against the noonday sun. Her shoulders stoop under the weight of the water jar. Her feet trudge, stirring dust on the path. She keeps her eyes down so she can dodge the stares of the others.

She is a Samaritan; she knows the sting of racism. She is a woman; she's bumped her head on the ceiling of sexism. She's been married to five men. Five. Five different marriages. Five different beds. Five different rejections. She knows the sound of slamming doors.

She knows what it means to love and receive no love in return. Her current mate won't even give her his name. He only gives her a place to sleep.

If there is a Grace Llewellen Smith in the New Testament, it is this woman. The epitaph of insignificance could have been hers. And it would have been, except for an encounter with a stranger.

On this particular day, she came to the well at noon. Why hadn't she gone in the early morning with the other women? Maybe she had. Maybe she just needed an extra draw of water on a hot day. Or maybe not. Maybe it was the other women she was avoiding. A walk in the hot sun was a small price to pay in order to escape their sharp tongues.

"Here she comes."

"Have you heard? She's got a new man!"

"They say she'll sleep with anyone."

"Shhh. There she is."

So she came to the well at noon. She expected silence. She expected solitude. Instead, she found one who knew her better than she knew herself.

He was seated on the ground: legs outstretched, hands folded, back resting against the well. His eyes were closed. She stopped and looked at him. She looked around. No one was near. She looked back at him. He was obviously Jewish. What was he doing here? His eyes opened and hers ducked in embarrassment. She went quickly about her task.

Sensing her discomfort, Jesus asked her for water. But she was too streetwise to think that all he wanted was a drink. "Since when does an uptown fellow like you ask a girl like me for water?" She wanted to know what he really had in mind. Her intuition was partly correct. He was interested in more than water. He was interested in her heart.

They talked. Who could remember the last time a man had spoken to her with respect?

He told her about a spring of water that would quench not the thirst of the throat, but of the soul.

That intrigued her. "Sir, give me this water so that I won't get thirsty and have to keep coming here to draw water."

"Go, call your husband and come back."

Her heart must have sunk. Here was a Jew who didn't care if she was a Samaritan. Here was a man who didn't look down on her as a woman. Here was the closest thing to gentleness she'd ever seen. And now he was asking her about . . . that.

Anything but that. Maybe she considered lying. "Oh, my husband? He's busy." Maybe she wanted to change the subject. Perhaps she wanted to leave—but she stayed. And she told the truth.

"I have no husband." (Kindness has a way of inviting honesty.)

You probably know the rest of the story. I wish you didn't. I wish you were hearing it for the first time. For if you were, you'd be wide eyed as you waited to see what Jesus would do next. Why? Because you've wanted to do the same thing.

You've wanted to take off your mask. You've wanted to stop pretending. You've wondered what God would do if you opened your cobweb-covered door of secret sin.

This woman wondered what Jesus would do. She must have wondered if the kindness would cease when the truth was revealed. *He will be angry. He will leave. He will think I'm worthless.*

If you've had the same anxieties, then get out your pencil. You'll want to underline Jesus' answer.

"You're right. You have had five husbands and the man you are with now won't even give you a name."

No criticism? No anger? No what-kind-of-mess-have-you-made-of-your-life lectures?

No. It wasn't perfection that Jesus was seeking, it was honesty.

The woman was amazed.

"I can see that you are a prophet." Translation? "There is something different about you. Do you mind if I ask you something?"

Then she asked the question that revealed the gaping hole in her soul.

"Where is God? My people say he is on the mountain. Your people say he is in Jerusalem. I don't know where he is."

I'd give a thousand sunsets to see the expression on Jesus' face as he heard those words. Did his eyes water? Did he smile? Did he look up into the clouds and wink at his father? Of all the places to find a hungry heart—Samaria?

Of all the Samaritans to be searching for God—a woman?

Of all the women to have an insatiable appetite for God—a five-time divorcée?

And of all the people to be chosen to personally receive the secret of the ages, an outcast among outcasts? The most "insignificant" person in the region?

Remarkable. Jesus didn't reveal the secret to King Herod. He didn't request an audience of the Sanhedrin and tell them the news. It wasn't within the colonnades of a Roman court that he announced his identity.

No, it was in the shade of a well in a rejected land to an ostracized woman. His eyes must have danced as he whispered the secret.

"I am the Messiah."

The most important phrase in the chapter is one easily overlooked. "The woman left her water jar beside the well and ran back to the village, telling everyone, 'Come and see a man who told me everything I ever did! Could he possibly be the Messiah?'" (John 4:28–29 NLT)

Don't miss the drama of the moment. Look at her eyes, wide with amazement. Listen to her as she struggles for words. "Y-y-y-you a-a-a-are the M-m-m-messiah!" And watch as she scrambles to her feet, takes one last look at this grinning Nazarene, turns and runs right into the burly chest of Peter. She almost falls, regains her balance, and hotfoots it toward her hometown.

Did you notice what she forgot? She forgot her water jar. She left behind the jug that had caused the sag in her shoulders. She left behind the burden she brought.

Suddenly the shame of the tattered romances disappeared. Suddenly the insignificance of her life was swallowed by the significance of the moment. "God is here! God has come! God cares . . . for me!"

That is why she forgot her water jar. That is why she ran to the city. That is why she grabbed the first person she saw and announced her discovery, "I just talked to a man who knows everything I ever did . . . and he loves me anyway!"

The disciples offered Jesus some food. He refused it—he was too excited! He had just done what he does best. He had taken a life that was drifting and given it direction.

He was exuberant!

"Look!" he announced to disciples, pointing at the woman who was running to the village. "Vast fields of human souls are ripening all around us, and are ready now for the reaping" (John 4:35 TLB).

Who could eat at a time like this?

For some of you the story of these two women is touching but distant. You belong. You are needed and you know it. You've got more friends than you can visit and more tasks than you can accomplish.

Insignificance will not be chiseled on your tombstone.

Be thankful.

But others of you are different. You paused at the epitaph because it was yours. You see the face of Grace Smith when you look into the mirror. You know why the Samaritan woman was avoiding people. You do the same thing.

You know what it's like to have no one sit by you at the cafeteria. You've wondered what it would be like to have one good friend. You've been in love and you wonder if it is worth the pain to do it again.

And you, too, have wondered where in the world God is.

I have a friend named Joy who teaches underprivileged children in an inner city church. Her class is a lively group of nine-year-olds who love life and aren't afraid of God. There is one exception, however—a timid girl by the name of Barbara.

Her difficult home life had left her afraid and insecure. For the weeks that my friend was teaching the class, Barbara never spoke. Never. While the other children talked, she sat. While the others sang, she was silent. While the others giggled, she was quiet.

Always present. Always listening. Always speechless.

Until the day Joy gave a class on heaven. Joy talked about seeing God. She talked about tearless eyes and deathless lives.

Barbara was fascinated. She wouldn't release Joy from her stare.

She listened with hunger. Then she raised her hand. "Mrs. Joy?"

Joy was stunned. Barbara had never asked a question. "Yes, Barbara?"

"Is heaven for girls like me?"

Again, I would give a thousand sunsets to have seen Jesus' face as this tiny prayer reached his throne. For indeed that is what it was—a prayer.

An earnest prayer that a good God in heaven would remember a forgotten soul on earth. A prayer that God's grace would seep into the cracks and cover one the church let slip through. A prayer to take a life that no one else could use and use it as no one else could.

Not a prayer from a pulpit, but one from a bed in a convalescent home. Not a prayer prayed confidently by a black-robed seminarian, but one whispered fearfully by a recovering alcoholic.

A prayer to do what God does best: take the common and make it spectacular. To once again take the rod and divide the sea. To take a pebble and kill a Goliath. To take water and make sparkling wine. To take a peasant boy's lunch and feed a multitude. To take mud and restore sight. To take three spikes and a wooden beam and make them the hope of humanity. To take a rejected woman and make her a missionary.

· ———

There are two graves in this chapter. The first is the lonely one in the Locke Hill Cemetery. The grave of Grace Llewellen Smith. She knew not love. She knew not gratification. She knew only the pain of the chisel as it carved this epitaph into her life.

> *Sleeps, but rests not.*
> *Loved, but was loved not.*
> *Tried to please, but pleased not.*
> *Died as she lived—alone.*

That, however, is not the only grave in this story. The second is near a water well. The tombstone? A water jug. A forgotten water jug. It has no words, but has great significance—for it is the burial place of insignificance.

FOR REFLECTION AND DISCUSSION

1. If you were to write an epitaph for yourself that expresses your current lot in life, what would it say?

2. Read John 4:4–42. How did Jesus use his own needs as tools for evangelism (vv. 6–15)? What can we learn from this? What is the "living water" Jesus talks about in verse 10? What does it do?

3. Identify the single greatest lesson you have learned from this story of the Samaritan Woman.

4. Sit down with a close friend or your spouse and write out what gives your life purpose and meaning. Be specific. The next time you are overwhelmed by the rising tides of futility, take out that list and read it.

5. Do you know any Grace Llewellen Smiths? What can you do to help make them feel more significant? Why not do it today?

Chapter 6

MARY, MARTHA, AND LAZARUS

They had a dinner for Jesus. Martha served the food, and Lazarus was one of the people eating with Jesus. Mary brought in a pint of very expensive perfume made from pure nard. She poured the perfume on his feet, and then she wiped his feet with her hair. And the sweet smell from the perfume filled the whole house.

{ JOHN 12:2–3 }

YOUR PLACE IN GOD'S BAND

Two of my teenage years were spent carrying a tuba in my high school marching band. My mom wanted me to learn to read music, and the choir was full while the band was a tuba-tooter short, so I signed up. Not necessarily what you would describe as a call from God, but it wasn't a wasted experience either.

I had a date with a twirler.

I learned to paint white shoe polish on school buses.

I learned that when you don't know your music, you need to put your lips to the horn and pretend you do rather than play and remove all doubt.

And I learned some facts about harmony that I'll pass on to you.

I marched next to the bass-drum player. What a great sound. *Boom. Boom. Boom.* Deep, cavernous, thundering. At the right measure in the right music, there is nothing better than the sound of a bass drum. *Boom. Boom. Boom.*

And at the end of my flank marched the flute section. Oh, how their music soared. Whispering, lifting, rising into the clouds.

Ahead of me, at the front of my line, was our first-chair trumpet. A band member through and through. While some guys shot hoops and others drove hot rods, he played the trumpet. And it showed. Put him on the fifty yard line and let him blow. He could raise the spirit. He could raise the flag. He could have raised the roof on the stadium if we'd had one.

Flute and trumpets sound very different. (See? I told you I learned a lot in band.) The flute whispers. The trumpet shouts. The flute comforts. The trumpet bugles. There's nothing like a trumpet—in limited dosages. A person can only be blasted at for so long. After a while you need to hear something softer. Something sweeter. You need to hear a little flute. But even the sound of the flute can go flat if there is no rhythm or cadence. That's why you also need the drum.

But who wants the drum all by itself? Ever seen a band made up of bass drums? Would you attend a concert of a hundred drums? Probably not. But what band would want to be without a bass drum or flute or trumpet?

> The soft flute
>> needs
>>> the brash trumpet
>>> needs
>>>> the steady drum
>>>> needs
>>>>> the soft flute
>>>>> needs
>>>>>> the brash trumpet.

Get the idea? The operative word is *need*. They need each other.

By themselves they make music. But together, they make magic.

Now, what I saw two decades ago in the band, I see today in the church. We need each other. Not all of us play the same instrument. Some believers are lofty, and others are solid. Some keep the pace while others lead the band. Not all of us make the same sound. Some are soft, and others are loud. And not all of us have the same ability. Some need to be on the fifty yard line raising the flag. Others need to be in the background playing backup. But each of us has a place.

Some play the drums (like Martha).

Some play the flute (like Mary).

And others sound the trumpet (like Lazarus).

Mary, Martha, and Lazarus were like family to Jesus. After the Lord raised Lazarus from the dead, they decided to give a dinner for Jesus. They decided to honor him by having a party on his behalf (see John 12:2).

They didn't argue over the best seat. They didn't resent each other's abilities. They didn't try to outdo each other. All three worked together with one purpose. But each one fulfilled that purpose in his or her unique manner. Martha served; she always kept everyone in step. Mary worshiped; she anointed her Lord with an extravagant gift, and its aroma filled the air. Lazarus had a story to tell, and he was ready to tell it.

Three people, each one with a different skill, a different ability. But each one of equal value. Think about it. Could their family have done without one of the three?

Could we do without one of the three today?

Every church needs a Martha. Change that. Every church needs a hundred Marthas. Sleeves rolled and ready, they keep the pace for the church. Because of Marthas, the church budget gets balanced, the church babies get bounced, and the church building gets built. You don't appreciate Marthas until a Martha is missing, and then all the Marys and Lazaruses are scrambling around looking for the keys and the thermostats and the overhead projectors.

Marthas are the Energizer bunnies of the church. They keep going and going and going. They store strength like a camel stores water. Since they don't seek the spotlight, they don't live off the applause. That's not to say they don't need it. They just aren't addicted to it.

Marthas have a mission. In fact, if Marthas have a weakness, it is their tendency to elevate the mission over the Master. Remember when Martha did that? A younger Martha invites a younger Jesus to come for dinner. Jesus accepts and brings his disciples.

The scene Luke describes has Mary seated and Martha fuming. Martha is angry because Mary is, horror of horrors, sitting at the feet of Jesus. How impractical! How irrelevant! How unnecessary! I mean, who has time to sit and listen when there is bread to be baked, tables to be set, and souls to be saved? So Martha complained, "Lord, don't you care that my sister has left me alone to do all the work? Tell her to help me" (Luke 10:40).

My, my! Aren't we testy? All of a sudden Martha has gone from serving Jesus to making demands of Jesus. The room falls silent. The disciples duck their eyes. Mary flushes red. And Jesus speaks. He speaks not only to Martha of Bethany, but to all Marthas who tend to think that a bass drum is the only instrument in the band.

"Martha, Martha, you are worried and upset about many things. Only one thing is important. Mary has chosen the better thing, and it will never be taken away from her" (Luke 10:41–42).

Apparently Martha got the point, for later we find her serving again.

> Here a dinner was given in Jesus' honor. Martha served, while Lazarus was among those reclining at the table with him. Then Mary took about a pint of pure nard, an expensive perfume; she poured it on Jesus' feet and wiped his feet with her hair. And the house was filled with the fragrance of the perfume. (John 12:2–3 NIV)

Is Mary in the kitchen? No, she is playing her flute for Jesus. She is worshiping, for that is what she loves to do. But this time Martha doesn't object. She has learned that there is a place for praise and worship, and that is what Mary is doing. And what is Mary's part in the dinner? She brings a pint of very expensive perfume and pours it on Jesus' feet, then wipes his feet with her hair. The smell of the perfume fills the house, just like the sound of praise can fill a church.

An earlier Martha would have objected. Such an act was too lavish, too extravagant, too generous. But this mature Martha has learned that just as there is a place in the kingdom of God for sacrificial service, there is also a place for extravagant praise.

Marys are gifted with praise. They don't just sing; they worship. They don't simply attend church; they go to offer praise. They don't just talk about Christ; they radiate Christ.

Marys have one foot in heaven and the other on a cloud. It's not easy for them to come to earth, but sometimes they need to. Sometimes they need to be reminded that there are bills to be paid and classes to be taught.

But don't remind them too harshly. Flutes are fragile. Marys are precious souls with tender hearts. If they have found a place at the foot of Jesus, don't ask them to leave. Much better to ask them to pray for you.

That's what I do. When I find a Mary (or a Michael), I'm quick to ask, "How do I get on your prayer list?"

Every church desperately needs some Marys.

We need them to pray for our children.

We need them to put passion in our worship.

We need them to write songs of praise and sing songs of glory.

We need them to kneel and weep and lift their hands and pray.

We need them because we tend to forget how much God loves worship. Marys don't forget. They know that God wants to be known as a father. They know that a father likes nothing more than to have his children sit as his feet and spend time with him.

Marys are good at that.

They, too, must be careful. They must meditate often on Luke 6:46. "Why do you call me 'Lord, Lord,' but do not do what I say?"

Marys need to remember that service is worship.

Marthas need to remember that worship is service.

And Lazarus? He needs to remember that not everyone can play the trumpet.

You see, as far as we know, Lazarus did nothing at the dinner. He saved his actions for outside the house. Read carefully John 12:9:

A large crowd of Jews heard that Jesus was in Bethany. So they went there to see not only Jesus, but Lazarus, whom Jesus raised from the dead. So the leading priests made plans to kill Lazarus, too. Because of Lazarus many Jews were leaving them and believing in Jesus.

Wow! Because of Lazarus many Jews were "believing in Jesus." Lazarus has been given a trumpet. He has a testimony to give—and what a testimony he has!

"I was always a good fellow," he would say. "I paid my bills. I loved my sisters. I even enjoyed being around Jesus. But I wasn't one of the followers. I didn't get as close as Peter and James and those guys. I kept my distance. Nothing personal. I just didn't want to get carried away.

"But then I got sick. And then I died. I mean, I died dead.

"Nothing left. Stone-cold. No life. No breath. Nothing. I died to everything. I saw life from the tomb. And then Jesus called me from the grave. When he spoke, my heart beat and my soul stirred, and I was alive again. And I want you to know he can do the same for you."

God gave Martha a bass drum of service. God gave Mary a flute for praise. And God gave Lazarus a trumpet. And he stood on center stage and played it.

God still gives trumpets. God still calls people from the pits. God still gives pinch-me-I'm-dreaming, too-good-to-be-true testimonies. But not everyone has a dramatic testimony. Who wants a band full of trumpets?

Some convert the lost. Some encourage the saved. And some keep the movement in step. All are needed.

If God has called you to be a Martha, then serve! Remind the rest of us that there is evangelism in feeding the poor and there is worship in nursing the sick.

If God has called you to be a Mary, then worship! Remind the rest of us that we don't have to be busy to be holy. Urge us with your example to put down our clipboards and megaphones and be quiet in worship.

If God has called you to be a Lazarus, then testify. Remind the rest of us that we, too, have a story to tell. We, too, have neighbors who are lost. We, too, have died and been resurrected.

Each of us has our place at the table.

Except one. There was one at Martha's house who didn't find his place. Though he had been near Jesus longer than any of the others, he was furthest in his faith. His name was Judas. He was a thief. When Mary poured the perfume he feigned spirituality. "The perfume could have been sold and given to the poor," he said. But Jesus knew Judas's heart, and Jesus defended Mary's worship. Years later, John, too, knew Judas's heart, and John explained that Judas was a thief (John 12:6). And all these years he had been dipping his hand in the treasury. The reason he wanted the perfume to be sold and the money put in the treasury was so that he could get his hands on it.

What a sad ending to a beautiful story. But what an appropriate ending. For in every church there are those like Martha who take time to serve. There are those like Mary who take time to worship. There are those like Lazarus who take time to testify.

And there are those like Judas who take, take, take, and never give in return. Are you a Judas? I ask the question carefully, yet honestly. Are you near Christ but far from his heart? Are you at the dinner with a sour soul? Are you always criticizing the gifts of others yet seldom, if ever, giving your own? Are you benefiting from the church while never giving to it? Do others give sacrificially while you give miserly? Are you a Judas?

Do you take, take, take, and never give? If so, you are the Judas in this story.

If you are a Martha, be strengthened. God sees your service.

If you are a Mary, be encouraged. God receives your worship.

If you are a Lazarus, be strong. God honors your conviction.

But if you are a Judas, be warned. God sees your selfishness.

For Reflection and Discussion

1. Are you more like a Martha, a Mary, or a Lazarus? Explain.
2. Describe some of the Marthas, Marys, and Lazaruses in your church.
3. "Marys need to remember that service is worship. Marthas need to remember that worship is service. And Lazarus? He needs to remember that not everyone can play the trumpet." How can service be worship? How can worship be service?
4. Are you satisfied with how you're fitting in with God's band? Why or why not?
5. Read Romans 12:4–8. What does this passage teach us about unity? What does it teach us about diversity? What does it teach us about the relationship of the two?

Chapter 7

ABIGAIL

Abigail flew into action. She took two hundred loaves of bread, two skins of wine, five sheep dressed out and ready for cooking, a bushel of roasted grain, a hundred raisin cakes, and two hundred fig cakes, and she had it all loaded on some donkeys. Then she said to her young servants, "Go ahead and pave the way for me. I'm right behind you." But she said nothing to her husband Nabal.

As she was riding her donkey, descending into a ravine, David and his men were descending from the other end, so they met there on the road. David had just said, "That sure was a waste, guarding everything this man had out in the wild so that nothing he had was lost—and now he rewards me with insults. A real slap in the face! May God do his worst to me if Nabal and every cur in his misbegotten brood aren't dead meat by morning!"

As soon as Abigail saw David, she got off her donkey and fell on her knees at his feet, her face to the ground in homage, saying, "My master, let me take the blame! Let me speak to you. Listen to what I have to say. Don't dwell on what that brute Nabal did. He acts out the meaning of his name: Nabal, Fool. Foolishness oozes from him.

"I wasn't there when the young men my master sent arrived. I didn't see them. And now, my master, as God lives and as you live, God has kept you from this avenging murder—and may your enemies, all who seek my master's harm, end up like Nabal! Now take this gift that I, your servant girl, have brought to my master, and give it to the young men who follow in the steps of my master. . . .

And David said, "Blessed be God, the God of Israel. He sent you to meet me! And blessed be your good sense! Bless you for keeping me from murder and taking charge of looking out for me. A close call! As God lives, the God of Israel who kept me from hurting you, if you had not come as quickly as you did, stopping me in my tracks, by morning there would have been nothing left of Nabal but dead meat."

Then David accepted the gift she brought him and said, "Return home in peace. I've heard what you've said and I'll do what you've asked."

{ 1 SAM. 25:18–25, 32–35 MSG }

BARBARIC BEHAVIOR

Ernest Gordon groans in the Death House of Chungkai, Burma. He listens to the moans of the dying and smells the stench of the dead. Pitiless jungle heat bakes his skin and parches his throat. Had he the strength, he could wrap one hand around his bony thigh. But he has neither the energy nor the interest. Diphtheria has drained both; he can't walk; he can't even feel his body. He shares a cot with flies and bedbugs and awaits a lonely death in a Japanese prisoner-of-war camp.

How harsh the war has been on him. He entered World War II in his early twenties, a robust Highlander in Scotland's Argyle and Sutherland Brigade. But then came the capture by the Japanese, months of back-breaking labor in the jungle, daily beatings, and slow starvation. Scotland seems forever away. Civility, even farther.

The Allied soldiers behave like barbarians, stealing from each other, robbing dying colleagues, fighting for food scraps. Servers shortchange rations so they can have extra for themselves. The law of the jungle has become the law of the camp.

Gordon is happy to bid it adieu. Death by disease trumps life in Chungkai. But then something wonderful happens. Two new prisoners, in whom hope still stirs, are transferred to the camp. Though also sick and frail, they heed a higher code. They share their meager meals and volunteer for extra work. They cleanse Gordon's ulcerated sores and massage his atrophied legs. They give him his first bath in six weeks. His strength slowly returns and, with it, his dignity.

Their goodness proves contagious, and Gordon contracts a case. He begins to treat the sick and share his rations. He even gives away his few belongings. Other soldiers do likewise. Over time, the tone of the camp softens and brightens. Sacrifice replaces selfishness. Soldiers hold worship services and Bible studies.

Twenty years later, when Gordon served as chaplain of Princeton University, he described the transformation with these words:

> Death was still with us—no doubt about that. But we were slowly being freed from its destructive grip. . . . Selfishness, hatred . . . and pride were all anti-life. Love . . . self-sacrifice . . . and faith, on the other hand, were the essence of life . . . gifts of God to men. . . . Death no longer had the last word at Chungkai.[1]

Selfishness, hatred, and pride—you don't have to go to a POW camp to find them. A dormitory will do just fine. As will the boardroom of a corporation or the bedroom of a marriage or the backwoods of a county. The code of the jungle is alive and well. *Every man for himself. Get all you can, and can all you get. Survival of the fittest.*

Does the code contaminate your world? Do personal possessive pronouns dominate the language of your circle? *My* career, *my* dreams, *my* stuff. I want things to go *my* way on *my* schedule. If so, you know how savage this giant can be. Yet, every so often, a diamond glitters in the mud. A comrade shares, a soldier cares, or Abigail, stunning Abigail, stands on your trail.

She lived in the days of David and was married to Nabal, whose name means "fool" in Hebrew. He lived up to the definition.

Think of him as the Saddam Hussein of the territory. He owned cattle and sheep and took pride in both. He kept his liquor cabinet full, his date life hot, and motored around in a stretch limo. His NBA seats were front row, his jet was Lear, and he was prone to hop over to Vegas for a weekend of Texas Hold 'em. Half a dozen linebacker-size security guards followed him wherever he went.

Nabal needed the protection. He was "churlish and ill-behaved—a real Calebbite dog. . . . He is so ill-natured that one cannot speak to him"

(1 Sam. 25:3, 17)[2] He learned people skills in the local zoo. He never met a person he couldn't anger or a relationship he couldn't spoil. Nabal's world revolved around one person—Nabal. He owed nothing to anybody and laughed at the thought of sharing with anyone.

Especially David.

David played a Robin Hood role in the wilderness. He and his six hundred soldiers protected the farmers and shepherds from brigands and Bedouins. Israel had no highway patrol or police force, so David and his mighty men met a definite need in the countryside. They guarded with enough effectiveness to prompt one of Nabal's shepherds to say, "Night and day they were a wall around us all the time we were herding our sheep near them" (25:16 NIV).

David and Nabal cohabited the territory with the harmony of two bulls in the same pasture. Both strong and strong-headed. It was just a matter of time before they collided.

Trouble began to brew after the harvest. With sheep sheared and hay gathered, it was time to bake bread, roast lamb, and pour wine. Take a break from the furrows and flocks and enjoy the fruit of the labor. As we pick up the story, Nabal's men are doing just that.

David hears of the gala and thinks his men deserve an invitation. After all, they've protected the man's crops and sheep, patrolled the hills and secured the valleys. They deserve a bit of the bounty. David sends ten men to Nabal with this request: "We come at a happy time, so be kind to my young men. Please give anything you can find for them and for your son David" (25:8).

Boorish Nabal scoffs at the thought:

Who is David, and who is the son of Jesse? There are many servants nowadays who break away each one from his master. Shall I then take my bread and my water and my meat that I have killed for my shearers, and give it to men when I do not know where they are from? (25:10–11 NKJV)

Nabal pretends he's never heard of David, lumping him in with runaway slaves and vagabonds. Such insolence infuriates the messengers, and they turn on their heels and hurry back to David with a full report.

David doesn't need to hear the news twice. He tells the men to form a posse. Or, more precisely, "Strap on your swords!" (25:12 MSG).

Four hundred men mount up and take off. Eyes glare. Nostrils flare. Lips snarl. Testosterone flows. David and his troops thunder down on Nabal, the scoundrel, who obliviously drinks beer and eats barbecue with his buddies. The road rumbles as David grumbles, "May God do his worst to me if Nabal and every cur in his misbegotten brood aren't dead meat by morning!" (25:22 MSG).

Hang on. It's the Wild West in the Ancient East.

Then, all of a sudden, beauty appears. A daisy lifts her head in the desert; a swan lands at the meat packing plant; a whiff of perfume floats through the men's locker room. Abigail, the wife of Nabal, stands on the trail. Whereas he is brutish and mean, she is "intelligent and good-looking" (25:3 MSG).

Brains *and* beauty. Abigail puts both to work. When she learns of Nabal's crude response, she springs into action. With no word to her husband, she gathers gifts and races to intercept David. As David and his men descend a ravine, she takes her position, armed with "two hundred loaves of bread, two skins of wine, five sheep dressed out and ready for cooking, a bushel of roasted grain, a hundred raisin cakes, and two hundred fig cakes, . . . all loaded on some donkeys" (25:18 MSG).

Four hundred men rein in their rides. Some gape at the food; others gawk at the female. She's good lookin' with good cookin', a combination that stops any army. (Picture a neck-snapping blonde showing up at boot camp with a truck full of burgers and ice cream.)

Abigail's no fool. She knows the importance of the moment. She stands as the final barrier between her family and sure death. Falling at David's feet, she issues a plea worthy of a paragraph in Scripture. "On me, my lord, on me let this iniquity be! And please let your maidservant speak in your ears, and hear the words of your maidservant" (25:24 NKJV).

She doesn't defend Nabal but agrees that he is a scoundrel. She begs not for justice but forgiveness, accepting blame when she deserves none. "Please forgive the trespass of your maidservant" (25:28 NKJV). She offers the gifts from her house and urges David to leave Nabal to God and avoid the dead weight of remorse.

Her words fall on David like July sun on ice. He melts.

> Blessed be GOD, the God of Israel. He sent you to meet me! . . . A close call! . . . if you had not come as quickly as you did, stopping me in my tracks, by morning there would have been nothing left of Nabal but dead meat. . . . I've heard what you've said and I'll do what you've asked. (25:32–35 MSG)

David returns to camp. Abigail returns to Nabal. She finds him too drunk for conversation so waits until the next morning to describe how close David came to camp and Nabal came to death. "Right then and there he had a heart attack and fell into a coma. About ten days later GOD finished him off and he died" (25:37–38 MSG).

When David learns of Nabal's death and Abigail's sudden availability, he thanks God for the first and takes advantage of the second. Unable to shake the memory of the pretty woman in the middle of the road, he proposes, and she accepts. David gets a new wife, Abigail a new home, and we have a great principle: beauty can overcome barbarism.

Meekness saved the day that day. Abigail's gentleness reversed a river of anger. Humility has such power. Apologies can disarm arguments. Contrition can defuse rage. Olive branches do more good than battle-axes ever will. "Soft speech can break bones" (Prov. 25:15 NLT).

Abigail teaches so much. The contagious power of kindness. The strength of a gentle heart. Her greatest lesson, however, is to take our eyes from her beauty and set them on someone else's. She lifts our thoughts from a rural trail to a Jerusalem cross. Abigail never knew Jesus. She lived a thousand years before his sacrifice. Nevertheless, her story prefigures his life.

Abigail placed herself between David and Nabal. Jesus placed himself between God and us. Abigail volunteered to be punished for Nabal's sins. Jesus allowed heaven to punish him for yours and mine. Abigail turned away the anger of David. Didn't Christ shield you from God's?

He was our "Mediator who can reconcile God and humanity—the man Christ Jesus. He gave his life to purchase freedom for everyone" (1 Tim. 2:5–6 NLT). Who is a mediator but one who stands in between? And what did Christ do but stand in between God's anger and our punishment? Christ intercepted the wrath of heaven.

Something remotely similar happened at the Chungkai camp. One evening after work detail, a Japanese guard announced that a shovel was missing. The officer kept the Allies in formation, insisting that someone had stolen it. Screaming in broken English, he demanded that the guilty man step forward. He shouldered his rifle, ready to kill one prisoner at a time until a confession was made.

A Scottish soldier broke ranks, stood stiffly at attention, and said, "I did it." The officer unleashed his anger and beat the man to death. When the guard was finally exhausted, the prisoners picked up the man's body and their tools and returned to camp. Only then were the shovels recounted. The Japanese soldier had made a mistake. No shovel was missing after all.[3]

Who does that? What kind of person would take the blame for something he didn't do?

When you find the adjective, attach it to Jesus. "God has piled all our sins, everything we've done wrong, on him, on him" (Isa. 53:6 MSG). God treated his innocent Son like the guilty human race, his Holy One like a lying scoundrel, his Abigail like a Nabal.

Christ lived the life we could not live and took the punishment we could not take to offer the hope we cannot resist. His sacrifice begs us to ask this question: if he so loved us, can we not love each other? Having been forgiven, can we not forgive? Having feasted at the table of grace, can we not share a few crumbs? "My dear, dear friends, if God loved us like this, we certainly ought to love each other" (1 John 4:11 MSG).

Do you find your Nabal world hard to stomach? Then do what David did: stop staring at Nabal. Shift your gaze to Christ. Look more at the Mediator and less at the troublemakers. "Don't let evil get the best of you; get the best of evil by doing good" (Rom. 12:21 MSG). One prisoner can change a camp. One Abigail can save a family. Be the beauty amidst your beasts and see what happens.

FOR REFLECTION AND DISCUSSION

1. Describe a time you saw the good influence of one person change the atmosphere of a group or organization.
2. What specific environment could you reshape by your good influence?
3. How could you be the "beauty" that brings peace to a tense or combative situation? What would you hope to accomplish?
4. Read Proverbs 15:1. Which half of this verse did Nabal demonstrate? Which half of this verse did Abigail demonstrate? Which half of this verse do you normally demonstrate?
5. Think of a person whom you have injured, insulted, or alienated. Ask God to give you the grace and the humility to approach this person and ask for forgiveness. It may be tough, but pray that the Lord will bring peace and healing to the situation.

Chapter 8

❧

PARALYZED MAN

(With Cameo Appearances by Jonah, Daniel, and Joseph)

Afterward Jesus returned to Jerusalem for one of the Jewish holy days. Inside the city, near the Sheep Gate, was the pool of Bethesda, with five covered porches. Crowds of sick people—blind, lame, or paralyzed—lay on the porches. One of the men lying there had been sick for thirty-eight years. When Jesus saw him and knew he had been ill for a long time, he asked him, "Would you like to get well?"

"I can't, sir," the sick man said, "for I have no one to put me into the pool when the water bubbles up. Someone else always gets there ahead of me."

Jesus told him, "Stand up, pick up your mat, and walk!"

Instantly, the man was healed! He rolled up his sleeping mat and began walking!

{ JOHN 5:1–9, NLT }

BRIGHT LIGHTS ON DARK NIGHTS

For the longest time this story didn't make any sense to me. I couldn't figure it out. It's about a man who has barely enough faith to stand on, but Jesus treats him as if he'd laid his son on the altar for God. Martyrs and apostles deserve such honor, but not some pauper who doesn't know Jesus when he sees him. Or so I thought.

For the longest time I thought Jesus was too kind. I thought the story was too bizarre. I thought the story was too good to be true. Then I realized something. This story isn't about an invalid in Jerusalem. This story is about you. It's about me. The fellow isn't nameless. He has a name—yours. He has a face—mine. He has a problem—just like ours.

Jesus encounters the man near a large pool north of the temple in Jerusalem. It's 360 feet long, 130 feet wide, and 75 feet deep. A colonnade with five porches overlooks the body of water. It's a monument of wealth and prosperity, but its residents are people of sickness and disease.

It's called Bethesda. It could be called Central Park, Metropolitan Hospital, or even Joe's Bar and Grill. It could be the homeless huddled beneath a downtown overpass. It could be Calvary Baptist. It could be any collection of hurting people.

An underwater spring caused the pool to bubble occasionally. The people believed the bubbles were caused by the dipping of angels' wings. They also believed that the first person to touch the water after the angel did would be healed. Did healing occur? I don't know. But I do know crowds of invalids came to give it a try.

Picture a battleground strewn with wounded bodies, and you see Bethesda. Imagine a nursing home overcrowded and understaffed, and you see the pool. Call to mind the orphans in Bangladesh or the abandoned in New Delhi, and you will see what people saw when they passed Bethesda. As they passed, what did they hear? An endless wave of groans. What did they witness? A field of faceless need. What did they do? Most walked past, ignoring the people.

But not Jesus. He is in Jerusalem for a feast. He is alone. He's not there to teach the disciples or to draw a crowd. The people need him—so he's there.

Can you picture it? Jesus walking among the suffering.

What is he thinking? When an infected hand touches his ankle, what does he do? When a blind child stumbles in Jesus' path, does he reach down to catch the child? When a wrinkled hand extends for alms, how does Jesus respond?

Whether the watering hole is Bethesda or Bill's Bar . . . how does God feel when people hurt?

It's worth the telling of the story if all we do is watch him walk. It's worth it just to know he even came. He didn't have to, you know. Surely there are more sanitary crowds in Jerusalem. Surely there are more enjoyable activities. After all, this is the Passover feast. It's an exciting time in the holy city. People have come from miles around to meet God in the temple.

Little do they know that God is with the sick.

Little do they know that God is walking slowly, stepping carefully between the beggars and the blind.

Little do they know that the strong young carpenter who surveys the ragged landscape of pain is God.

"When they suffered, he suffered also" Isaiah wrote (Isa. 63:9). On this day Jesus must have suffered much.

On this day Jesus must have sighed often as he walked along the poolside of Bethesda . . . and he sighs when he comes to you and me.

Remember, I told you this story was about us? Remember, I said I found our faces in the Bible? Well, here we are, filling the white space between the letters of verse 5: "A man was lying there who had been sick for thirty-eight years."

Maybe you don't like being described like that. Perhaps you'd rather find yourself in the courage of David or the devotion of Mary. We all would. But before you or I can be like them, we must admit we are like the paralytic. Invalids out of options. Can't walk. Can't work. Can't care for ourselves. Can't even roll down the bank to the pool to cash in on the angel water.

You may be holding this book with healthy hands and reading with strong eyes, and you can't imagine what you and this four-decade invalid have in common. How could he be you? What do we have in common with him?

Simple. Our predicament and our hope. What predicament? It is described in Hebrews 12:14: "Anyone whose life is not holy will never see the Lord."

That's our predicament: Only the holy will see God. Holiness is a prerequisite to heaven. Perfection is a requirement for eternity. We wish it weren't so. We act like it isn't so. We act like those who are "decent" will see God. We suggest that those who try hard will see God. We act as if we're good if we never do anything too bad. And that goodness is enough to qualify us for heaven.

Sounds right to us, but it doesn't sound right to God. And he sets the standard. And the standard is high. "You must be perfect, just as your Father in heaven is perfect" (Matt. 5:48).

You see, in God's plan, God is the standard for perfection. We don't compare ourselves to others; they are just as fouled up as we are. The goal is to be like him; anything less is inadequate.

That's why I say the invalid is you and me. We, like the invalid, are paralyzed. We, like the invalid, are trapped. We, like the invalid, are stuck; we have no solution for our predicament.

That's you and me lying on the ground. That's us wounded and weary. When it comes to healing our spiritual condition, we don't have a chance. We might as well be told to pole-vault the moon. We don't have what it takes to be healed. Our only hope is that God will do for us what he did for the man at Bethesda—that he will step out of the temple and step into our ward of hurt and helplessness.

Which is exactly what he has done.

Read slowly and carefully Paul's description of what God has done for you: "When you were spiritually dead because of your sins and because you were not free from the power of your sinful self, God made you alive with Christ, and he forgave all our sins. He canceled the debt, which listed all the rules we failed to follow. He took away that record with its rules and nailed it to the cross. God stripped the spiritual rulers and powers of their authority. With the cross, he won the victory and showed the world that they were powerless" (Col. 2:13–15).

As you look at the words above, answer these questions. Who is doing the work? You or God? Who is active? You or God? Who is doing the saving? You or God? Who is the one with strength? And who is the one paralyzed?

Let's isolate some phrases and see. First, look at your condition. "When you were spiritually dead . . . and . . . you were not free."

The invalid was better off than we are. At least he was alive. Paul says that if you and I are outside of Christ, then we are dead. Spiritually dead. Corpses. Lifeless. Cadavers. Dead. What can a dead person do? Not much.

But look what God can do with the dead.

"God made you alive."

"God forgave."

"He canceled the debt."

"He took away that record."

"God stripped the spiritual rulers."

"He won the victory."

"[He] showed the world."

Again, the question. Who is active? You and I—or God? Who is trapped and who comes to the rescue?

God has thrown life jackets to every generation.

Look at Jonah in the fish belly—surrounded by gastric juices and sucked-in seaweed. For three days God has left him there. For three days Jonah has pondered his choices. And for three days he has come to the same conclusion: He ain't got one. From where he sits (or floats) there are two exits—and neither are very appealing. But then again, neither is Jonah. He blew it as a preacher. He was a flop as a fugitive. At best he's a coward, at worst a traitor. And what he's lacked all along he now has in abundance—guts.

So Jonah does the only thing he can do: He prays. He says nothing about how good he is—but a lot about how good God is. He doesn't even ask for help, but help is what he gets. Before he can say amen, the belly convulses, the fish belches, and Jonah lands face first on the beach.

Look at Daniel in the lions' den; his prospects aren't much better than Jonah's. Jonah had been swallowed, and Daniel is about to be. Flat on his back with the lions' faces so close he can smell their breath. The biggest one puts a paw on Daniel's chest and leans down to take the first bite and . . . nothing happens. Instead of a chomp, there is a bump. Daniel looks down and sees the nose of another lion rubbing against his belly. The lion's lips are snarling, but his mouth isn't opening.

That's when Daniel hears the snickering in the corner. He doesn't know who the fellow is, but he sure is bright and he sure is having fun. In his hands is a roll of bailing wire and on his face is one of those gotcha-while-you-weren't-watching expressions.

Or look at Joseph in the pit, a chalky hole in a hot desert. The lid has been pulled over the top and the wool has been pulled over his eyes. Those are his brothers up there, laughing and eating as if they did nothing more than tell him to get lost (which is what they'd done for most of his life). Those are his brothers, the ones who have every intention of leaving him to spend his days with the spiders and the snakes and then to die in the pit.

Like Jonah and Daniel, Joseph is trapped. He is out of options. There is no exit. There is no hope. But because Jacob's boys are as greedy as they were mean, Joseph is sold to some southbound gypsies and he changes history. Though the road to the palace takes a detour through a prison, it eventually ends up at the throne. And Joseph eventually stands before his brothers—this time with their asking for his help. And he is wise enough to give them what they ask and not what they deserve.

Or look at Barabbas on death row. The final appeal has been heard. The execution has been scheduled. Barabbas passes the time playing solitaire in his cell. He's resigned to the fact that the end is near. Doesn't appeal. Doesn't implore. Doesn't demand. The decision has been made, and Barabbas is going to die.

Like Jonah, Daniel, and Joseph, it's all over but the crying. And like Jonah, Daniel, and Joseph, the time to cry never comes. The steps of the warden echo in the chamber. Barabbas thinks he's bringing handcuffs and a final cigarette. Wrong. The warden brings street clothes. And Barabbas leaves the prison a free man because someone he'd probably never even seen took his place.

Such are the stories in the Bible. One near-death experience after another. Just when the neck is on the chopping block, just when the noose is around the neck, Calvary comes.

Angels pound on Lot's door—Genesis 19.

The whirlwind speaks to Job's hurt—Job 38–42.

The Jordan purges Naaman's plague—2 Kings 5.

An angel appears in Peter's cell—Acts 12.

God's efforts are strongest when our efforts are useless.

Go back to Bethesda for a moment. I want you to look at the brief but revealing dialogue between the paralytic and the Savior. Before Jesus heals him, he asks him a question: "Do you want to be well?"

"Sir, there is no one to help me get into the pool when the water starts moving. While I am coming to the water, someone else always gets in before me" (v. 7).

Is the fellow complaining? Is he feeling sorry for himself? Or is he just stating the facts? Who knows? But before we think about it too much, look what happens next.

"'Stand up. Pick up your mat and walk.'"

"And immediately the man was well; he picked up his mat and began to walk."

I wish we would do that; I wish we would take Jesus at his word. I wish, like heaven, that we would learn that when he says something, it happens. What is this peculiar paralysis that confines us? What is this stubborn unwillingness to be healed? When Jesus tells us to stand, let's stand.

When he says we're forgiven, let's unload the guilt.

When he says we're valuable, let's believe him.

When he says we're eternal, let's bury our fear.

When he says we're provided for, let's stop worrying.

When he says, "Stand up," let's do it.

I love the story of the private who ran after and caught the runaway horse of Napoleon. When he brought the animal back to the emperor, Napoleon thanked him by saying, "Thank you, Captain."

With one word the private was promoted. When the emperor said it, the private believed it. He went to the quartermaster, selected a new uniform, and put it on. He went to the officers' quarters and selected a bunk. He went to the officers' mess and had a meal.

Because the emperor said it, he believed it. Would that we would do the same.

Is this your story? It can be. All the elements are the same. A gentle stranger has stepped into your hurting world and offered you a hand.

Now it's up to you to take it.

FOR REFLECTION AND DISCUSSION

1. How often do you deliberately choose to be among the suffering? Is Jesus' presence at the pool of Bethesda an encouragement to you or a rebuke—or both? Explain.

2. In what way is the sick man's story really a tale about you and me?

3. Max writes, "We must admit we are like the paralytic. Invalids out of options." What does he mean by this? Do you agree with him? Why or why not?

4. Read Colossians 2:13–15. List the things Jesus accomplished for you on the Cross, based on this passage.

5. Is Jesus telling you today, like the paralytic, to "stand up" in any area of your life? If so, what? If he is, what do you plan to do about it?

Chapter 9

❧

JOHN

Mary said, "They have taken the Lord out of the tomb, and we don't know where they have put him."

So Peter and the other follower started for the tomb. They were both running, but the other follower ran faster than Peter and reached the tomb first. He bent down and looked in and saw the strips of linen cloth lying there, but he did not go in. Then following him, Simon Peter arrived and went into the tomb and saw the strips of linen lying there. He also saw the cloth that had been around Jesus' head, which was folded up and laid in a different place from the strips of linen. Then the other follower, who had reached the tomb first, also went in. He saw and believed.

{ JOHN 20:2–8 }

I CAN TURN YOUR
TRAGEDY INTO TRIUMPH

What do you say we have a chat about graveclothes? Sound like fun? Sound like a cheery topic? Hardly. Make a list of depressing subjects, and burial garments is somewhere between IRS audits and long-term dental care.

No one likes graveclothes. No one discusses graveclothes. Have you ever spiced up dinner-table chat with the question, "What are you planning to wear in your casket?" Have you ever seen a store specializing in burial garments? (If there is one, I have an advertising slogan to suggest: "Clothes to die for.")

Most folks don't discuss graveclothes.

The apostle John, however, was an exception. Ask him, and he'll tell you how he came to see burial garments as a symbol of triumph. He didn't always see them that way. A tangible reminder of the death of his best friend, Jesus, they used to seem like a symbol of tragedy. But on the first Easter Sunday, God took clothing of death and made it a symbol of life.

Could he do the same for you?

We all face tragedy. What's more, we've all received the symbols of tragedy. Yours might be a telegram from the war department, an ID bracelet from the hospital, a scar, or a court subpoena. We don't like these symbols, nor do we want these symbols. Like wrecked cars in a junkyard, they clutter up our hearts with memories of bad days.

Could God use such things for something good? How far can we go with verses like this one: "In everything God works for the good of those who love him" (Rom. 8:28)? Does "everything" include tumors and tests and tempers and terminations? John would answer yes. John would tell you that *God can turn any tragedy into a triumph, if only you will wait and watch.*

To prove his point, he would tell you about one Friday in particular.

Later, Joseph from Arimathea asked Pilate if he could take the body of Jesus. (Joseph was a secret follower of Jesus, because he was afraid of some of the leaders.) Pilate gave his permission, so Joseph came and took Jesus' body away. Nicodemus, who earlier had come to Jesus at night, went with Joseph. He brought about seventy-five pounds of myrrh and aloes. These two men took Jesus' body and wrapped it with the spices in pieces of linen cloth, which is how they bury the dead. (John 19:38–40)

Reluctant during Christ's life but courageous at his death, Joseph and Nicodemus came to serve Jesus. They came to bury him. They ascended the hill bearing the burial clothing.

Pilate had given his permission.

Joseph of Arimathea had given a tomb.

Nicodemus had brought the spices and linens.

John states that Nicodemus brought seventy-five pounds of myrrh and aloes. The amount is worth noting, for such a quantity of burial ointments was typically used only for kings. John also comments on the linens because to him they were a picture of Friday's tragedy. As long as there were no graveclothes, as long as there was no tomb, as long as there was no coroner, there was hope. But the arrival of the hearse triggered the departure of any hope. And to this apostle, the graveclothes symbolized tragedy.

Could there have been a greater tragedy for John than a dead Jesus? Three years earlier John had turned his back on his career and cast his lot with this Nazarene carpenter. Earlier in the week John had enjoyed a ticker-tape parade as Jesus and the disciples entered Jerusalem. Oh, how quickly things had turned! The people who had called him king on Sunday called for his death the following Friday. These linens were a tangible reminder that his friend and his future were wrapped in cloth and sealed behind a rock.

John didn't know on that Friday what you and I now know. He didn't know that Friday's tragedy would be Sunday's triumph. John would later confess that he "did not yet understand from the Scriptures that Jesus must rise from the dead" (John 20:9).

That's why what he did on Saturday is so important.

We don't know anything about this day; we have no passage to read, no knowledge to share. All we know is this: When Sunday came, John was still present. When Mary Magdalene came looking for him, she found him.

Jesus was dead. The Master's body was lifeless. John's friend and future were buried. But John had not left. Why? Was he waiting for the resurrection? No. As far as he knew, the lips were forever silent and the hands forever still. He wasn't expecting a Sunday surprise. Then why was he here?

You'd think he would have left. Who was to say that the men who crucified Christ wouldn't come after him? The crowds were pleased with one crucifixion; the religious leaders might have called for more. Why didn't John get out of town?

Perhaps the answer was pragmatic; perhaps he was taking care of Jesus' mother. Or perhaps he didn't have anywhere else to go. Could be he didn't have any money or energy or direction . . . or all of the above.

Or maybe he lingered because he loved Jesus.

To others, Jesus was a miracle worker. To others, Jesus was a master teacher. To others, Jesus was the hope of Israel. But to John, he was all of these and more. To John, Jesus was a friend.

You don't abandon a friend—not even when that friend is dead. John stayed close to Jesus.

He had a habit of doing this. He was close to Jesus in the upper room. He was close to Jesus in the Garden of Gethsemane. He was at the foot of the cross at the crucifixion, and he was a quick walk from the tomb at the burial.

Did he understand Jesus? No.

Was he glad Jesus did what he did? No.

But did he leave Jesus? No.

What about you? When you're in John's position, what do you do? When it's Saturday in your life, how do you react? When you are somewhere between yesterday's tragedy and tomorrow's triumph, what do you do? Do you leave God—or do you linger near him?

John chose to linger. And because he lingered on Saturday, he was around on Sunday to see the miracle.

Mary said, "They have taken the Lord out of the tomb, and we don't know where they have put him."

So Peter and the other follower started for the tomb. They were both running, but the other follower ran faster than Peter and reached the tomb first. He bent down and looked in and saw the strips of linen cloth lying there, but he did not go in. Then following him, Simon Peter arrived and went into the tomb and saw the strips of linen lying there. He also saw the cloth that had been around Jesus' head, which was folded up and laid in a different place from the strips of linen. Then the other follower, who had reached the tomb first, also went in. He saw and believed. (John 20:2–8)

Very early on Sunday morning Peter and John were given the news: "Jesus' body is missing!" Mary was urgent, both with her announcement and her opinion. She thought Jesus' enemies had taken his body away. Instantly the two disciples hurried to the sepulcher, John outrunning Peter and arriving first. What he saw so stunned him he froze at the entrance.

What did he see? "Strips of linen cloth." He saw "the cloth that had been around Jesus' head . . . folded up and laid in a different place from the strips of linen." He saw "cloth lying."

The original Greek provides helpful insight here. John employs a term that means "rolled up,"[1] "still in their folds."[2] These burial wraps had not been ripped off and thrown down. They were still in their original state! The linens were undisturbed. The graveclothes were still rolled and folded.

How could this be?

If friends had removed the body, would they not have taken the clothes with it?

If foes had taken the body, would they not have done the same?

If not, if for some reason friends or foes had unwrapped the body, would they have been so careful as to dispose of the clothing in such an orderly fashion? Of course not!

But if neither friend nor foe took the body, who did?

This was John's question, and this question led to John's discovery. "He saw and believed" (John 20:8).

Through the rags of death, John saw the power of life. Odd, don't you think, that God would use something as sad as a burial wrap to change a life?

But God is given to such practices:

In his hand empty wine jugs at a wedding become a symbol of power.

The coin of a widow becomes a symbol of generosity.

A crude manger in Bethlehem is his symbol of devotion.

And a tool of death is a symbol of his love.

Should we be surprised that he takes the wrappings of death and makes them the picture of life?

Which takes us back to the question. Could God do something similar in your life? Could he take what today is a token of tragedy and turn it into a symbol of triumph?

He did for my friend Rafael Rosales. Rafael is a minister in El Salvador. The Salvadoran guerrillas viewed him as an enemy of their movement and tried to kill him. Left to die in a burning automobile, Rafael escaped the car and the country. But he couldn't escape the memories. The scars would not let him.

Every glance in the mirror reminded him of his tormentors' cruelty.

He might have never recovered had the Lord not spoken to his heart. "They did the same to me" he heard his Savior say. And as God ministered to Rafael, Rafael began to see his scars differently. Rather than serve as a reminder of his own pain, they became a picture of his Savior's sacrifice. In time he was able to forgive his attackers. During the very week that I write these words, he is visiting his country, looking for a place to plant a new church.

Could such a change happen to you? I have no doubt. You simply need to do what John did. Don't leave. Hang around.

Remember the second half of the passage. "God works for the good of *those who love him*" (Rom. 8:28, italics mine). That's how John felt about Jesus. He loved him. He didn't understand him or always agree with him, but he loved him.

And because he loved him, he stayed near him.

The Bible says that "in everything God works for the good of those who love him." Before we close this chapter, do this simple exercise. Remove the word *everything,* and replace it with the symbol of your tragedy. For the apostle John, the verse would read: "In *burial clothing* God works for the good of those who love him." For Rafael it would read: "In *scars* God works for the good of those who love him."

How would Romans 8:28 read in your life?

In hospital stays God works for the good.

In divorce papers God works for the good.

In a prison term God works for the good.

If God can change John's life through a tragedy, could it be he will use a tragedy to change yours?

As hard as it may be to believe, you could be only a Saturday away from a resurrection. You could be only hours from that precious prayer of a changed heart, "God, did you do this for me?"

FOR REFLECTION AND DISCUSSION

1. "When it's Saturday in your life, how do you react?" What does Max mean by "Saturday in your life?" After tragedy strikes, do you leave God or linger near him? Explain.

2. Read John 19:38–40; 20:3–9. What did Peter and "the other disciple" (John, NIV) find when they entered the empty tomb on the day of Jesus' resurrection? Why did what they saw cause John to believe?

3. Read Romans 8:28. What does this verse say we "know"?

4. Follow through on Max's suggestion: "Do this simple exercise. Remove the word *everything* [in Romans 8:28], and replace it with the symbol of your tragedy." What happens when you do this?

5. On your own or with someone else, think of several stories in the Bible in which God took what appeared to be a clear defeat for his people and turned it into a triumph. In what area of your life could you use such a triumph right now? Enlist a friend to pray with you that God would engineer just such a reversal on your behalf.

Chapter 10

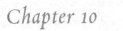

PAUL

So Saul headed toward Damascus. As he came near the city, a bright light from heaven suddenly flashed around him. Saul fell to the ground and heard a voice saying to him, "Saul, Saul! Why are you persecuting me?"

Saul said, "Who are you, Lord?"

The voice answered, "I am Jesus, whom you are persecuting. Get up now and go into the city. Someone there will tell you what you must do."

I have been near death many times. Five times the Jews have given me their punishment of thirty-nine lashes with a whip. Three different times I was beaten with rods. One time I was almost stoned to death. Three times I was in ships that wrecked, and one of those times I spent a night and a day in the sea. I have gone on many travels and have been in danger from rivers, thieves, my own people, the Jews, and those who are not Jews. I have been in danger in cities, in places where no one lives, and on the sea. And I have been in danger with false Christians. I have done hard and tiring work, and many times I did not sleep. I have been hungry and thirsty, and many times I have been without food. I have been cold and without clothes.

{ ACTS 9:3–6; 2 COR. 11:23–27 }

HIDDEN HEROES

True heroes are hard to identify. They don't look like heroes. Here's an example.

Step with me into a dank dungeon in Judea. Peer through the door's tiny window. Consider the plight of the man on the floor. He has just inaugurated history's greatest movement. His words have triggered a revolution that will span two millenniums. Future historians will describe him as courageous, noble, and visionary.

At this moment he appears anything but. Cheeks hollow. Beard matted. Bewilderment etched on his face. He leans back against the cold wall, closes his eyes, and sighs.

John had never known doubt. Hunger, yes. Loneliness, often. But doubt? Never. Only raw conviction, ruthless pronouncements, and rugged truth. Such was John the Baptist. Conviction as fierce as the desert sun.

Until now. Now the sun is blocked. Now his courage wanes. Now the clouds come. And now, as he faces death, he doesn't raise a fist of victory; he raises only a question. His final act is not a proclamation of courage, but a confession of confusion: "Find out if Jesus is the Son of God or not."

The forerunner of the Messiah is afraid of failure. *Find out if I've told the truth. Find out if I've sent people to the right Messiah. Find out if I've been right or if I've been duped.*[1]

Doesn't sound too heroic, does he?

We'd rather John die in peace. We'd rather the trailblazer catch a glimpse of the mountain. Seems only right that the sailor be granted a sighting of the shore. After all, didn't Moses get a view of the valley? Isn't John the cousin of Jesus? If anybody deserves to see the end of the trail, doesn't he?

Apparently not.

The miracles he prophesied, he never saw. The kingdom he announced, he never knew. And the Messiah he proclaimed, he now doubts.

John doesn't look like the prophet who would be the transition between law and grace. He doesn't look like a hero.

Heroes seldom do.

Can I take you to another prison for a second example?

This time the jail is in Rome. The man is named Paul. What John did to present Christ, Paul did to explain him. John cleared the path; Paul erected signposts.

Like John, Paul shaped history. And like John, Paul would die in the jail of a despot. No headlines announced his execution. No observer recorded the events. When the ax struck Paul's neck, society's eyes didn't blink. To them Paul was a peculiar purveyor of an odd faith.

Peer into the prison and see him for yourself: bent and frail, shackled to the arm of a Roman guard. Behold the apostle of God. Who knows when his back last felt a bed or his mouth knew a good meal? Three decades of travel and trouble, and what's he got to show for it?

There's squabbling in Phillipi, competition in Corinth, the legalists are swarming in Galatia. Crete is plagued by money-grabbers. Ephesus is stalked by womanizers. Even some of Paul's own friends have turned against him.

Dead broke. No family. No property. Nearsighted and worn out.

Oh, he had his moments. Spoke to an emperor once, but couldn't convert him. Gave a lecture at an Areopagus men's club, but wasn't asked to speak there again. Spent a few days with Peter and the boys in Jerusalem, but they couldn't seem to get along, so Paul hit the road.

And never got off. Ephesus, Thessalonica, Athens, Syracuse, Malta. The only list longer than his itinerary was his misfortune. Got stoned in one city and stranded in another. Nearly drowned as many times as he nearly starved. If he spent more than one week in the same place, it was probably a prison.

He never received a salary. Had to pay his own travel expenses. Kept a part-time job on the side to make ends meet.

Doesn't look like a hero.

Doesn't sound like one either. He introduced himself as the worst sinner in history. He was a Christian-killer before he was a Christian leader. At times his heart was so heavy, Paul's pen drug itself across the page. "What a miserable man I am! Who will save me from this body that brings me death?" (Rom. 7:24).

Only heaven knows how long he stared at the question before he found the courage to defy logic and write, "I thank God for saving me through Jesus Christ our Lord!" (Rom. 7:25).

One minute he's in charge; the next he's in doubt. One day he's preaching; the next he's in prison. And that's where I'd like you to look at him. Look at him in the prison.

Pretend you don't know him. You're a guard or a cook or a friend of the hatchet man, and you've come to get one last look at the guy while they sharpen the blade.

What you see shuffling around in his cell isn't too much. But what I lean over and tell you is: "That man will shape the course of history."

You chuckle, but I continue.

"Nero's fame will fade in this man's light."

You turn and stare. I continue.

"His churches will die. But his thoughts? Within two hundred years his thoughts will influence the teaching of every school on this continent."

You shake your head.

"See those letters? Those letters scribbled on parchment? They'll be read in thousands of languages and will impact every major creed and constitution of the future. Every major figure will read them. Every single one."

That would be your breaking point. "No way. He's an old man with an odd faith. He'll be killed and forgotten before his head hits the floor."

Who could disagree? What rational thinker would counter? Paul's name would blow like the dust his bones would become.

Just like John's. No level-headed observer would think otherwise. Both were noble, but passing. Courageous, but small. Radical, yet unnoticed. No one—I repeat, no one—bade farewell to these men thinking their names would be remembered more than a generation.

Their peers simply had no way of knowing—and neither do we.

For that reason, a hero could be next door and you wouldn't know it. The fellow who changes the oil in your car could be one. A hero in coveralls? Maybe. Maybe as he works he prays, asking God to do with the heart of the driver what he does with the engine.

The day-care worker where you drop off the kids? Perhaps. Perhaps her morning prayers include the name of each child and the dream that one of them will change the world. Who's to say God isn't listening?

The parole officer downtown? Could be a hero. She could be the one who challenges the ex-con to challenge the teens to challenge the gangs.

I know, I know. These folks don't fit our image of a hero. They look too, too . . . well, normal. Give us four stars, titles, and headlines. But something tells me that for every hero in the spotlight, there are dozens in the shadows. They don't get press. They don't draw crowds. They don't even write books!

But behind every avalanche is a snowflake.

Behind a rock slide is a pebble.

An atomic explosion begins with one atom.

And a revival can begin with one sermon.

History proves it. John Egglen had never preached a sermon in his life. Never.

Wasn't that he didn't want to, just never needed to. But then one morning he did. The snow left his town of Colchester, England, buried in white. When he awoke on that January Sunday in 1850, he thought of staying home. Who would go to church in such weather?

But he reconsidered. He was, after all, a deacon. And if the deacons didn't go, who would? So he put on his boots, hat, and coat and walked the six miles to the Methodist Church.

He wasn't the only member who considered staying home. In fact, he was one of the few who came. Only thirteen people were present. Twelve members and one visitor. Even the minister was snowed in. Someone suggested they go home. Egglen would hear none of that. They'd come this far; they would have a service. Besides, they had a visitor. A thirteen-year-old boy.

But who would preach? Egglen was the only deacon. It fell to him.

And so he did. His sermon lasted only ten minutes. It drifted and wandered and made no point in an effort to make several. But at the end, an uncharacteristic courage settled upon the man. He lifted his eyes and looked straight at the boy and challenged: "Young man, look to Jesus. Look! Look! Look!"

Did the challenge make a difference? Let the boy, now a man, answer. "I did look, and then and there the cloud on my heart lifted, the darkness rolled away, and at that moment I saw the sun."

The boy's name? Charles Haddon Spurgeon. England's prince of preachers.[2]

Did Egglen know what he'd done? No.

Do heroes know when they are heroic? Rarely.

Are historic moments acknowledged when they happen?

You know the answer to that one. (If not, a visit to the manger will remind you.) We seldom see history in the making, and we seldom recognize heroes. Which is just as well, for if we knew either, we might mess up both.

But we'd do well to keep our eyes open. Tomorrow's Spurgeon might be mowing your lawn. And the hero who inspires him might be nearer than you think.

He might be in your mirror.

FOR REFLECTION AND DISCUSSION

1. In what way do heroes seldom look like heroes? What's your picture of a hero?

2. What "heroes out of the spotlight" do you know? What makes them heroes?

3. Have you been a hero to anyone? Could you be a hero to anyone?

4. Read Mark 1:1–8. How would you describe John in modern terms? How did his appearance and lifestyle help him accomplish his mission? In what way was he a hero?

5. Read 2 Corinthians 4:7–11: 6:4–10; 11:22–28. What do you learn about Paul from these passages? What in them describes the kind of hero he was? Do these passages encourage or discourage you? Why?

Chapter 11

❧

TWO
CRIMINALS

There were also two criminals led out with Jesus to be put to death. When they came to a place called the Skull, the soldiers crucified Jesus and the criminals—one on his right and the other on his left. . . .

One of the criminals on a cross began to shout insults at Jesus: "Aren't you the Christ? Then save yourself and us."

But the other criminal stopped him and said, "You should fear God! You are getting the same punishment he is. We are punished justly, getting what we deserve for what we did. But this man has done nothing wrong." Then he said, "Jesus, remember me when you come into your kingdom."

Jesus said to him, "I tell you the truth, today you will be with me in paradise."

{ LUKE 23:32-33, 39-43 }

I WILL LET YOU CHOOSE

M eet Edwin Thomas, a master of the stage. During the latter half of the 1800s, this small man with the huge voice had few rivals. Debuting in *Richard III* at the age of fifteen, he quickly established himself as a premier Shakespearean actor. In New York he performed *Hamlet* for one hundred consecutive nights. In London he won the approval of the tough British critics. When it came to tragedy on the stage, Edwin Thomas was in a select group.

When it came to tragedy in life, the same could be said as well.

Edwin had two brothers, John and Junius. Both were actors, although neither rose to his stature. In 1863, the three siblings united their talents to perform *Julius Caesar.* The fact that Edwin's brother John took the role of Brutus was an eerie harbinger of what awaited the brothers—and the nation—two years hence.

For this John who played the assassin in *Julius Caesar* is the same John who took the role of assassin in Ford's Theatre. On a crisp April night in 1865, he stole quietly into the rear of a box in the Washington theater and fired a bullet at the head of Abraham Lincoln. Yes, the last name of the brothers was Booth—Edwin Thomas Booth and John Wilkes Booth.

Edwin was never the same after that night. Shame from his brother's crime drove him into retirement. He might never have returned to the stage had it not been for a twist of fate at a New Jersey train station. Edwin was awaiting his coach when a well-dressed young man, pressed by the crowd, lost his footing and fell between the platform and a moving train. Without hesitation, Edwin locked a leg around a railing, grabbed the man, and pulled him to safety. After the sighs of relief, the young man recognized the famous Edwin Booth.

Edwin, however, didn't recognize the young man he'd rescued. That knowledge came weeks later in a letter, a letter he carried in his pocket to the grave. A letter from General Adams Budeau, chief secretary to General Ulysses S. Grant. A letter thanking Edwin Booth for saving the life of the child of an American hero, Abraham Lincoln. How ironic that while one brother killed the president, the other brother saved the president's son. The boy Edwin Booth yanked to safety? Robert Todd Lincoln.[1]

Edwin and James Booth. Same father, mother, profession, and passion—yet one chooses life, the other, death. How could it happen? I don't know, but it does. Though their story is dramatic, it's not unique.

Abel and Cain, both sons of Adam. Abel chooses God. Cain chooses murder. And God lets him.

Abraham and Lot, both pilgrims in Canaan. Abraham chooses God. Lot chooses Sodom. And God lets him.

David and Saul, both kings of Israel. David chooses God. Saul chooses power. And God lets him.

Peter and Judas, both deny their Lord. Peter seeks mercy. Judas seeks death. And God lets him.

In every age of history, on every page of Scripture, the truth is revealed: God allows us to make our own choices.

And no one delineates this more clearly than Jesus. According to him, we can choose:

a narrow gate or a wide gate (Matt. 7:13–14)
a narrow road or a wide road (Matt. 7:13–14)
the big crowd or the small crowd (Matt. 7:13–14)

We can choose to:

build on rock or sand (Matt. 7:24–27)
serve God or riches (Matt. 6:24)
be numbered among the sheep or the goats (Matt. 25:32–33)

"Then they [those who rejected God] will go away to eternal punishment, but the righteous to eternal life" (Matt. 25:46 NIV).

God gives eternal choices, and these choices have eternal consequences.

Isn't this the reminder of Calvary's trio? Ever wonder why there were two crosses next to Christ? Why not six or ten? Ever wonder why Jesus was in the center? Why not on the far right or far left? Could it be that the two crosses on the hill symbolize one of God's greatest gifts? The gift of choice.

The two criminals have so much in common. Convicted by the same system. Condemned to the same death. Surrounded by the same crowd. Equally close to the same Jesus. In fact, they begin with the same sarcasm: "The two criminals also said cruel things to Jesus" (Matt. 27:44 CEV).

But one changed.

> One of the criminals on a cross began to shout insults at Jesus: "Aren't you the Christ? Then save yourself and us." But the other criminal stopped him and said, "You should fear God! You are getting the same punishment he is. We are punished justly, getting what we deserve for what we did. But this man has done nothing wrong." Then he said, "Jesus, remember me when you come into your kingdom." Jesus said to him, "I tell you the truth, today you will be with me in paradise." (Luke 23:39–43)

Much has been said about the prayer of the penitent thief, and it certainly warrants our admiration. But while we rejoice at the thief who changed, dare we forget the one who didn't? *What about him, Jesus? Wouldn't a personal invitation be appropriate? Wouldn't a word of persuasion be timely?*

Does not the shepherd leave the ninety-nine sheep and pursue the one lost? Does not the housewife sweep the house until the lost coin is found? Yes, the shepherd does, the housewife does, but the father of the prodigal, remember, does nothing.

The sheep was lost innocently.

The coin was lost irresponsibly.

But the prodigal son left intentionally.

The father gave him the choice. Jesus gave both criminals the same.

There are times when God sends thunder to stir us. There are times when God sends blessings to lure us. But then there are times when God sends nothing but silence as he honors us with the freedom to choose where we spend eternity.

And what an honor it is! In so many areas of life we have no choice. Think about it. You didn't choose your gender. You didn't choose your siblings. You didn't choose your race or place of birth.

Sometimes our lack of choices angers us. "It's not fair," we say. It's not fair that I was born in poverty or that I sing so poorly or that I run so slowly. But the scales of life were forever tipped on the side of fairness when God planted a tree in the Garden of Eden. All complaints were silenced when Adam and his descendants were given free will, the freedom to make whatever eternal choice we desire. Any injustice in this life is offset by the honor of choosing our destiny in the next.

Wouldn't you agree? Would you have wanted otherwise? Would you have preferred the opposite? You choose everything in this life, and he chooses where you spend the next? You choose the size of your nose, the color of your hair, and your DNA structure, and he chooses where you spend eternity? Is that what you would prefer?

It would have been nice if God had let us order life like we order a meal. I'll take good health and a high IQ. I'll pass on the music skills, but give me a fast metabolism . . . Would've been nice. But it didn't happen. When it came to your life on earth, you weren't given a voice or a vote.

But when it comes to life after death, you were. In my book that seems like a good deal. Wouldn't you agree?

Have we been given any greater privilege than that of choice? Not only does this privilege offset any injustice, the gift of free will can offset any mistakes.

Think about the thief who repented. Though we know little about him, we know this: He made some bad mistakes in life. He chose the wrong crowd, the wrong morals, the wrong behavior. But would you consider his life a waste? Is he spending eternity reaping the fruit of all the bad choices he made? No, just the opposite. He is enjoying the fruit of the one good choice he made. In the end all his bad choices were redeemed by a solitary good one.

You've made some bad choices in life, haven't you? You've chosen the wrong friends, maybe the wrong career, even the wrong spouse. You look back over your life and say, "If only . . . if only I could make up for those bad choices." You can. One good choice for eternity offsets a thousand bad ones on earth.

The choice is yours.

How can two brothers be born of the same mother, grow up in the same home, and one choose life and the other choose death? I don't know, but they do.

How could two men see the same Jesus and one choose to mock him and the other choose to pray to him? I don't know, but they did.

And when one prayed, Jesus loved him enough to save him. And when the other mocked, Jesus loved him enough to let him.

He allowed him the choice.

He does the same for you.

FOR REFLECTION AND DISCUSSION

1. Why do you think God allows us to make our own choices?
2. What "big" choices are facing you right now? How will you make them?
3. "God gives eternal choices, and these choices have eternal consequences." What does Max mean by "eternal choices"?
4. "There are times when God sends thunder to stir us. There are times when God sends blessings to lure us. But then there are times when God sends nothing but silence as he honors us with the freedom to choose where we spend eternity." Describe a time when God sent thunder to stir you. Has God ever sent blessings to lure you? Explain. Why would God be silent when we're faced with such a huge choice?
5. Read Deuteronomy 30:19–20 and Joshua 24:14–15. What choices are presented in these passages? Who is to do the choosing? What choice have you made in this crucial area of life? Explain.

Chapter 12

❧

MOSES

One day Moses was taking care of Jethro's flock. (Jethro was the priest of Midian and also Moses' father-in-law.) When Moses led the flock to the west side of the desert, he came to Sinai, the mountain of God. There the angel of the LORD appeared to him in flames of fire coming out of a bush. Moses saw that the bush was on fire, but it was not burning up. So he said, "I will go closer to this strange thing. How can a bush continue burning without burning up?"

When the LORD saw Moses was coming to look at the bush, God called to him from the bush, "Moses, Moses!"

And Moses said, "Here I am."

Then God said, "Do not come any closer. Take off your sandals, because you are standing on holy ground. I am the God of your ancestors—the God of Abraham, the God of Isaac, and the God of Jacob.". . .

The LORD said . . . "I have heard the cries of the people of Israel, and I have seen the way the Egyptians have made life hard for them. So now I am sending you to the king of Egypt. Go! Bring my people, the Israelites, out of Egypt!"

{ EX. 3:1–6, 9–10 }

THE VOICE FROM
THE MOP BUCKET

The hallway is silent except for the wheels of the mop bucket and the shuffle of the old man's feet. Both sound tired.

Both know these floors. How many nights has Hank cleaned them? Always careful to get in the corners. Always careful to set up his yellow caution sign warning of wet floors. Always chuckling as he does. "Be careful everyone," he laughs to himself, knowing no one is near.

Not at three a.m.

Hank's health isn't what it used to be. Gout keeps him awake. Arthritis makes him limp. His glasses are so thick his eyeballs look twice their size. Shoulders stoop. But he does his work. Slopping soapy water on linoleum. Scrubbing the heel marks left by the well-heeled lawyers. He'll be finished an hour before quitting time. Always finishes early. Has for twenty years.

When finished he'll put away his bucket and take a seat outside the office of the senior partner and wait. Never leaves early. Could. No one would know. But he doesn't.

He broke the rules once. Never again.

Sometimes, if the door is open, he'll enter the office. Not for long. Just to look. The suite is larger than his apartment. He'll run his finger over the desk. He'll stroke the soft leather couch. He'll stand at the window and watch the gray sky turn gold. And he'll remember.

He once had such an office.

Back when Hank was Henry. Back when the custodian was an executive. Long ago. Before the night shift. Before the mop bucket. Before the maintenance uniform. Before the scandal.

Hank doesn't think about it much now. No reason to. Got in trouble, got fired, and got out. That's it. Not many people know about it. Better that way. No need to tell them.

It's his secret.

Hank's story, by the way, is true. I changed the name and a detail or two. I gave him a different job and put him in a different century. But the story is factual. You've heard it. You know it. When I give you his real name, you'll remember.

But more than a true story, it's a common story. It's a story of a derailed dream. It's a story of high hopes colliding with harsh realities.

Happens to all dreamers. And since all have dreamed, it happens to us all.

In Hank's case, it was a mistake he could never forget. A grave mistake. Hank killed someone. He came upon a thug beating up an innocent man, and Hank lost control. He killed the mugger. When word got out, Hank got out.

Hank would rather hide than go to jail. So he ran. The executive became a fugitive.

True story. Common story. Most stories aren't as extreme as Hank's. Few spend their lives running from the law. Many, however, live with regrets.

"I could have gone to college on a golf scholarship," a fellow told me just last week on the fourth tee box. "Had an offer right out of school. But I joined a rock-and-roll band. Ended up never going. Now I'm stuck fixing garage doors."

"Now I'm stuck." Epitaph of a derailed dream.

Pick up a high school yearbook and read the "What I want to do" sentence under each picture. You'll get dizzy breathing the thin air of mountaintop visions:

"Ivy league school."
"Write books and live in Switzerland."

"Physician in a Third World country."

"Teach inner-city kids."

Yet, take the yearbook to a twentieth-year reunion and read the next chapter. Some dreams have come true, but many haven't. Not that all should, mind you. I hope the little guy who dreamed of being a sumo wrestler came to his senses. And I hope he didn't lose his passion in the process. Changing direction in life is not tragic. Losing passion in life is.

Something happens to us along the way. Convictions to change the world downgrade to commitments to pay the bills. Rather than make a difference, we make a salary. Rather than look forward, we look back. Rather than look outward, we look inward.

And we don't like what we see.

Hank didn't. Hank saw a man who'd settled for the mediocre. Trained in the finest institutions of the world, yet working the night shift in a minimum-wage job so he wouldn't be seen in the day.

But all that changed when he heard the voice from the mop bucket. (Did I mention that his story is true?)

At first he thought the voice was a joke. Some of the fellows on the third floor play these kinds of tricks.

"Henry, Henry," the voice called.

Hank turned. No one called him Henry anymore.

"Henry, Henry."

He turned toward the pail. It was glowing. Bright red. Hot red. He could feel the heat ten feet away. He stepped closer and looked in. The water wasn't boiling.

"This is strange," Hank mumbled to himself as he took another step to get a closer look. But the voice stopped him.

"Don't come any closer. Take off your shoes. You are on holy tile."

Suddenly Hank knew who was speaking. "God?"

I'm not making this up. I know you think I am. Sounds crazy. Almost irreverent. God speaking from a hot mop bucket to a janitor named Hank? Would it be believable if I said God was speaking from a burning bush to a shepherd named Moses?

Maybe that one's easier to handle—because you've heard it before. But just because it's Moses and a bush rather than Hank and a bucket, it's no less spectacular.

It sure shocked the sandals off Moses. We wonder what amazed the old fellow more: that God spoke in a bush or that God spoke at all.

Moses, like Hank, had made a mistake.

You remember his story. Adopted nobility. An Israelite reared in an Egyptian palace. His countrymen were slaves, but Moses was privileged. Ate at the royal table. Educated in the finest schools.

But his most influential teacher had no degree. She was his mother. A Jewess who was hired to be his nanny. "Moses," you can almost hear her whisper to her young son, "God has put you here on purpose. Someday you will set your people free. Never forget, Moses. Never forget."

Moses didn't. The flame of justice grew hotter until it blazed. Moses saw an Egyptian beating a Hebrew slave. Just like Hank killed the mugger, Moses killed the Egyptian.

The next day Moses saw the Hebrew. You'd think the slave would say thanks. He didn't. Rather than express gratitude, he expressed anger. "Will you kill me too?" he asked (see Exod. 2:14).

Moses knew he was in trouble. He fled Egypt and hid in the wilderness. Call it a career shift. He went from dining with the heads of state to counting heads of sheep.

Hardly an upward move.

And so it happened that a bright, promising Hebrew began herding sheep in the hills. From the Ivy League to the cotton patch. From the Oval Office to a taxicab. From swinging a golf club to digging a ditch.

Moses thought the move was permanent. There is no indication he ever intended to go back to Egypt. In fact, there is every indication he wanted to stay with his sheep. Standing barefoot before the bush, he confessed, "I am not a great man! How can I go to the king and lead the Israelites out of Egypt?" (Exod. 3:11).

I'm glad Moses asked that question. It's a good one. Why Moses? Or, more specifically, why eighty-year-old Moses?

The forty-year-old version was more appealing. The Moses we saw in Egypt was brash and confident. But the Moses we find four decades later is reluctant and weather-beaten.

Had you or I looked at Moses back in Egypt, we would have said, "This man is ready for battle." Educated in the finest system in the world. Trained by the ablest soldiers. Instant access to the inner circle of the Pharaoh. Moses spoke their language and knew their habits. He was the perfect man for the job.

Moses at forty we like. But Moses at eighty? No way. Too old. Too tired. Smells like a shepherd. Speaks like a foreigner. What impact would he have on Pharaoh? He's the wrong man for the job.

And Moses would have agreed. "Tried that once before," he would say. "Those people don't want to be helped. Just leave me here to tend my sheep. They're easier to lead."

Moses wouldn't have gone. You wouldn't have sent him. I wouldn't have sent him.

But God did. How do you figure? Benched at forty and suited up at eighty. Why? What does he know now that he didn't know then? What did he learn in the desert that he didn't learn in Egypt?

The ways of the desert, for one. Forty-year-old Moses was a city boy. Octogenarian Moses knows the name of every snake and the location of every watering hole. If he's going to lead thousands of Hebrews into the wilderness, he better know the basics of Desert Life 101.

Family dynamics, for another. If he's going to be traveling with families for forty years, it might help to understand how they work. He marries a woman of faith, the daughter of a Midianite priest, and establishes his own family.

But more than the ways of the desert and the people, Moses needed to learn something about himself.

Apparently he has learned it. God says Moses is ready.

And to convince him, God speaks through a bush. (Had to do something dramatic to get Moses' attention.)

"School's out," God tells him. "Now it's time to get to work." Poor Moses. He didn't even know he was enrolled.

But he was. And, guess what? So are you. The voice from the bush is the voice that whispers to you. It reminds you that God is not finished with you yet. Oh, you may think he is. You may think you've peaked. You may think he's got someone else to do the job.

If so, think again.

"God began doing a good work in you, and I am sure he will continue it until it is finished when Jesus Christ comes again" (Phil. 1:6).

Did you see what God is doing? *A good work in you.*

Did you see when he will be finished? *When Jesus comes again.*

May I spell out the message? *God ain't finished with you yet.*

Your Father wants you to know that. And to convince you, he may surprise you. He may speak through a bush, a mop bucket, or stranger still, he may speak through this book.

FOR REFLECTION AND DISCUSSION

1. Have your convictions changed as you've grown older? If so, in what way? Do you like what you see? Explain.
2. Would you have given Moses the job of bringing Israel out of slavery? Explain.
3. What do you think God saw in Moses? What do you think he might see in you?
4. What do you think God may still be calling you to do?
5. Read Philippians 1:6. What promise is given in this verse? How can it change the way you live? Does it affect the way you live personally? Explain.

Chapter 13

⤡⤢

JOSEPH

Joseph's brothers saw him coming from far away. Before he reached them, they made a plan to kill him. They said to each other, "Here comes that dreamer. Let's kill him and throw his body into one of the wells. We can tell our father that a wild animal killed him. Then we will see what will become of his dreams."

But Reuben heard their plan and saved Joseph, saying, "Let's not kill him. Don't spill any blood. Throw him into this well here in the desert, but don't hurt him!" Reuben planned to save Joseph later and send him back to his father. So when Joseph came to his brothers, they pulled off his robe with long sleeves and threw him into the well. It was empty, and there was no water in it. . . .

So when the Midianite traders came by, the brothers took Joseph out of the well and sold him to the Ishmaelites for eight ounces of silver. And the Ishmaelites took him to Egypt. . . .

After Jacob died, Joseph's brothers said, "What if Joseph is still angry with us? We did many wrong things to him. What if he plans to pay us back?" So they sent a message to Joseph that said, "Your father gave this command before he died. He said to us, 'You have done wrong and have sinned and done evil to Joseph. Tell Joseph to forgive you, his brothers.' So now, Joseph, we beg you to forgive our wrong. We are the servants of the God of your father." When Joseph received the message, he cried.

And his brothers went to him and bowed low before him and said, "We are your slaves." Then Joseph said to them, "Don't be afraid. Can I do what only God can do? You meant to hurt me, but God turned your evil into good to save the lives of many people, which is being done."

{ GEN. 37:18–24, 28; 50:15–20 }

WHEN CRICKETS
MAKE YOU CRANKY

Forgive me if this chapter is disjointed. As I write, I am angry. I am angered by a cricket. He's loud. He's obnoxious. He's hidden. And he's in big trouble if I ever find him.

I arrived at my office early. Two hours before my alarm sounded, I was here. Sleeves rolled back and computer humming. *Beat the phones*, I thought. *Get a jump on the morning*, I planned. *Get a leg up on the day.*

But *Get your hands on that cricket* is what I keep mumbling.

Now, I have nothing against nature. The melody of a canary, I love. The pleasant hum of the wind in the leaves, I relish. But the predawn *raack-raack-raack* of a cricket bugs me.

So I get on my knees and follow the sound through the office. I peek under boxes. I pull books off the shelves. I get on my belly and look under my desk. Humbling. I've been sabotaged by a one-inch bug.

What is this insolent irritant that reduces a man to bug-stalker?

Finally, I isolate the culprit.

Rats, he's behind a shelf. Out of my reach. Hidden in a haven of plywood. I can't get to him. All I can do is throw pens at the base of the shelf. So I do. *Pop. Pop. Pop.* One after another. A barrage of Bics. He finally shuts up.

But the silence lasts only a minute.

So forgive me if my thoughts are fragmented, but I'm launching artillery every other paragraph. This is no way to work. This is no way to start the day. My floor is cluttered. My pants are dirty. My train of thought is derailed. I mean, how can you write about anger with a stupid bug in your office?

Oooops. Guess I'm in the right frame of mind after all . . .

Anger. This morning it's easy to define: the noise of the soul. *Anger.* The unseen irritant of the heart. *Anger.* The relentless invader of silence.

Just like the cricket, anger irritates.

Just like the cricket, anger isn't easily silenced.

Just like the cricket, anger has a way of increasing in volume until it's the only sound we hear. The louder it gets the more desperate we become.

When we are mistreated, our animalistic response is to go on the hunt. Instinctively, we double up our fists. Getting even is only natural. Which, incidentally, is precisely the problem. Revenge is natural, not spiritual. Getting even is the rule of the jungle. Giving grace is the rule of the kingdom.

Some of you are thinking, *Easy for you to say, Max, sitting there in your office with a cricket as your chief irritant. You ought to try living with my wife. Or, You ought to have to cope with my past. Or, You ought to raise my kids. You don't know how my ex has mistreated me. You don't have any idea how hard my life has been.*

And you're right, I don't. But I have a very clear idea how miserable your future will be unless you deal with your anger.

X-ray the soul of the vengeful and behold the tumor of bitterness: black, menacing, malignant. Carcinoma of the spirit. Its fatal fibers creep around the edge of the heart and ravage it. Yesterday you can't alter, but your reaction to yesterday you can. The past you cannot change, but your response to your past you can.

Impossible, you say? Let me try to show you otherwise.

Imagine you are from a large family—a dozen or so kids. A family more blended than the Brady bunch. All the children are from the same dad, but they have four or five different moms.

Imagine also that your dad is a sneak and has been one for a long time. Everybody knows it. Everybody knows he cheated your uncle out of the estate. Everybody knows he ran like a coward to avoid getting caught.

Let's also imagine that your great-uncle tricked your dad into marrying your mother's sister. He got your dad drunk before the wedding and had his ugly daughter go to the altar instead of the pretty one your dad thought he was marrying.

That didn't slow down your father, though. He just married them both. The one he loved couldn't have kids, so he slept with her maid. In fact, he had a habit of sleeping with most of the kitchen help; as a result, most of your siblings resemble the cooks.

Finally the bride your dad wanted to marry in the first place gets pregnant . . . and you are born.

You're the favored son . . . and your brothers know it.

You get a car. They don't. You get Armani; they get K-Mart. You get summer camp; they get summer jobs. You get educated; they get angry.

And they get even. They sell you to some foreign service project, put you on a plane for Egypt, and tell your dad you got shot by a sniper. You find yourself surrounded by people you don't know, learning a language you don't understand, and living in a culture you've never seen.

Imaginary tale? No. It's the story of Joseph. A favored son in a bizarre family, he had every reason to be angry.

He tried to make the best of it. He became the chief servant of the head of the Secret Service. His boss's wife tried to seduce him, and when he refused, she pouted and he ended up in prison. Pharaoh got wind of the fact that Joseph could interpret dreams and let him take a shot at some of Pharaoh's own.

When Joseph interpreted them he got promoted out of the prison into the palace as prime minister. The second highest position in all of Egypt. The only person Joseph bowed before was the king.

Meanwhile a famine hits and Jacob, Joseph's father, sends his sons to Egypt for a foreign loan. The brothers don't know it, but they are standing in front of the same brother they sold to the Gypsies some twenty-two years earlier.

They don't recognize Joseph, but Joseph recognizes them. A bit balder and paunchier, but they are the same brothers. Imagine Joseph's thoughts. The last time he saw these faces, he was looking up at them from the bottom of a pit. The last time he heard these voices, they were laughing at him. The last time they called his name, they called him every name in the book.

Now is his chance to get even. He has complete control. One snap of his fingers and these brothers are dead. Better yet, slap some manacles on their hands and feet and let them see what an Egyptian dungeon is like. Let them sleep in the mud. Let them mop floors. Let them learn Egyptian.

Revenge is within Joseph's power. And there is power in revenge. Intoxicating power.

Haven't we tasted it? Haven't we been tempted to get even?

As we escort the offender into the courtroom, we announce, "He hurt me!" The jurors shake their heads in disgust. "He abandoned me!" we explain, and the chambers echo with our accusation. "Guilty!" the judge snarls as he slams the gavel. "Guilty!" the jury agrees. "Guilty!" the audience proclaims. We delight in this moment of justice. We relish this pound of flesh. So we prolong the event. We tell the story again and again and again.

Now let's freeze-frame that scene. I have a question. Not for all of you, but for a few of you. Some of you are in the courtroom. The courtroom of complaint. Some of you are rehashing the same hurt every chance you get with anyone who will listen.

For you, I have this question: Who made you God? I don't mean to be cocky, but why are you doing his work for him?

"Vengeance is Mine," God declared. "I will repay" (Heb. 10:30 NKJV).

"Don't say, 'I'll pay you back for the wrong you did.' Wait for the LORD, and he will make things right" (Prov. 20:22).

Judgment is God's job. To assume otherwise is to assume God can't do it.

Revenge is irreverent. When we strike back we are saying, "I know

126

vengeance is yours, God, but I just didn't think you'd punish enough. I thought I'd better take this situation into my own hands. You have a tendency to be a little soft."

Joseph understands that. Rather than get even, he reveals his identity and has his father and the rest of the family brought to Egypt. He grants them safety and provides them a place to live. They live in harmony for seventeen years.

But then Jacob dies and the moment of truth comes. The brothers have a hunch that with Jacob gone they'll be lucky to get out of Egypt with their heads on their shoulders. So they go to Joseph and plead for mercy.

"Your father gave this command before he died. . . . 'Tell Joseph to forgive you'" (Gen. 50:16–17). (I have to smile at the thought of grown men talking like this. Don't they sound like kids, whining, "Daddy said to be nice to us"?)

Joseph's response? "When Joseph received the message, he cried" (Gen. 50:17). *"What more do I have to do?"* his tears implore. *"I've given you a home. I've provided for your families. Why do you still mistrust my grace?"*

Please read carefully the two statements he makes to his brothers. First he asks, "Can I do what only God can do?" (v. 19).

May I restate the obvious? Revenge belongs to God! If vengeance is God's, then it is not ours. God has not asked us to settle the score or get even. Ever.

Why? The answer is found in the second part of Joseph's statement: "You meant to hurt me, but God turned your evil into good to save the lives of many people, which is being done" (v. 20).

Forgiveness comes easier with a wide-angle lens. Joseph uses one to get the whole picture. He refuses to focus on the betrayal of his brothers without also seeing the loyalty of his God.

It always helps to see the big picture.

Some time ago I was in an airport lobby when I saw an acquaintance enter. He was a man I hadn't seen in a while but had thought about often.

He'd been through a divorce, and I was close enough to it to know that he deserved some of the blame.

I noticed he was not alone. Beside him was a woman. *Why, that scoundrel! Just a few months out and here he has another lady?*

Any thought of greeting him disappeared as I passed judgment on his character. But then he saw me. He waved at me. He motioned me over. I was caught. I was trapped. I'd have to go visit with the reprobate. So I did.

"Max, meet my aunt and her husband."

I gulped. I hadn't noticed the man.

"We're on our way to a family reunion. I know they would really like to meet you."

"We use your books in our home Bible study," my friend's uncle spoke up. "You've got some great insights."

"If only you knew," I said to myself. I had committed a common sin of the unforgiving. I had cast a vote without knowing the story.

To forgive someone is to admit our limitations. We've been given only one piece of life's jigsaw puzzle. Only God has the cover of the box.

To forgive someone is to display reverence. Forgiveness is not saying the one who hurt you was right. Forgiveness is stating that God is fair and he will do what is right.

After all, don't we have enough things to do without trying to do God's work too?

Guess what. I just noticed something. The cricket is quiet. I got so wrapped up in this chapter I forgot him. I haven't thrown a pen for an hour. Guess he fell asleep. Could be that's what he wanted to do all along, but I kept waking him up with my Bics.

He ended up getting some rest. I ended up finishing this chapter. Remarkable what gets accomplished when we let go of our anger.

For Reflection and Discussion

1. Does the "rule of the jungle" or the "rule of the kingdom" most often characterize your response to mistreatment? Give an example of how you react to mistreatment.
2. "When we strike back we are saying, 'I know vengeance is yours, God, but I just didn't think you'd punish enough. I thought I'd better take this situation into my own hands. You have a tendency to be a little soft.'" Have you ever felt this way? Explain.
3. How does forgiveness come easier with a "wide-angle lens"?
4. How is it made more difficult with a "telephoto lens"?
5. Read Proverbs 20:22. What negative command is given here? What positive command is given? How do the two work together?

Chapter 14

❧

DAVID

⌘

Early in the morning David left the flock with a shepherd, loaded up and set out, as Jesse had directed. He reached the camp as the army was going out to its battle positions, shouting the war cry. Israel and the Philistines were drawing up their lines facing each other. David left his things with the keeper of supplies, ran to the battle lines and greeted his brothers. As he was talking with them, Goliath, the Philistine champion from Gath, stepped out from his lines and shouted his usual defiance, and David heard it. When the Israelites saw the man, they all ran from him in great fear. . . .

David said to the Philistine, "You come against me with sword and spear and javelin, but I come against you in the name of the Lord Almighty, the God of the armies of Israel, whom you have defied. This day the Lord will hand you over to me, and I'll strike you down and cut off your head. Today I will give the carcasses of the Philistine army to the birds of the air and the beasts of the earth, and the whole world will know that there is a God in Israel. All those gathered here will know that it is not by sword or spear that the Lord saves; for the battle is the Lord's, and he will give all of you into our hands."

As the Philistine moved closer to attack him, David ran quickly toward the battle line to meet him. Reaching into his bag and taking out a stone, he slung it and struck the Philistine on the forehead. The stone sank into his forehead, and he fell facedown on the ground.

So David triumphed over the Philistine with a sling and a stone; without a sword in his hand he struck down the Philistine and killed him.

{ 1 SAM. 17:20–24, 45–50 NIV }

FACING YOUR GIANTS

The slender, beardless boy kneels by the brook. Mud moistens his knees. Bubbling water cools his hand. Were he to notice, he could study his handsome features in the water. Hair the color of copper. Tanned, sanguine skin and eyes that steal the breath of Hebrew maidens. He searches not for his reflection, however, but for rocks. Stones. Smooth stones. The kind that stack neatly in a shepherd's pouch, rest flush against a shepherd's leather sling. Flat rocks that balance heavy on the palm and missile with comet-crashing force into the head of a lion, a bear, or, in this case, a giant.

Goliath stares down from the hillside. Only disbelief keeps him from laughing. He and his Philistine herd have rendered their half of the valley into a forest of spears; a growling, bloodthirsty gang of hoodlums boasting do-rags, BO, and barbed-wire tattoos. Goliath towers above them all: nine feet, nine inches tall in his stocking feet, wearing 125 pounds of armor, and snarling like the main contender at the World Wrestling Federation championship night. He wears a size-20 collar, a 10 1/2 hat, and a 56-inch belt. His biceps burst, thigh muscles ripple, and boasts belch through the canyon. "This day I defy the ranks of Israel! Give me a man and let us fight each other" (1 Sam. 17:10 NIV). *Who will go mano a mano conmigo? Give me your best shot.*

No Hebrew volunteers. Until today. Until David.

David just showed up this morning. He clocked out of sheep watching to deliver bread and cheese to his brothers on the battlefront. That's where David hears Goliath defying God, and that's when David makes his decision. Then he takes his staff in his hand, and he chooses for himself five smooth stones from the brook and puts them in a shepherd's bag, in a pouch that he has, and his sling is in his hand. And he draws near to the Philistine (17:40).[1]

Goliath scoffs at the kid, nicknames him Twiggy. "Am I a dog, that you come to me with sticks?" (17:43 NASB). Skinny, scrawny David. Bulky, brutish Goliath. The toothpick versus the tornado. The minibike attacking the eighteen-wheeler. The toy poodle taking on the rottweiler. What odds do you give David against his giant?

Better odds, perhaps, than you give yourself against yours.

Your Goliath doesn't carry sword or shield; he brandishes blades of unemployment, abandonment, sexual abuse, or depression. Your giant doesn't parade up and down the hills of Elah; he prances through your office, your bedroom, your classroom. He brings bills you can't pay, grades you can't make, people you can't please, whiskey you can't resist, pornography you can't refuse, a career you can't escape, a past you can't shake, and a future you can't face.

You know well the roar of Goliath.

David faced one who foghorned his challenges morning and night. "For forty days, twice a day, morning and evening, the Philistine giant strutted in front of the Israelite army" (17:16 NLT). Yours does the same. First thought of the morning, last worry of the night—your Goliath dominates your day and infiltrates your joy.

How long has he stalked you? Goliath's family was an ancient foe of the Israelites. Joshua drove them out of the Promised Land three hundred years earlier. He destroyed everyone except the residents of three cities: Gaza, Gath, and Ashdod. Gath bred giants like Yosemite grows sequoias. Guess where Goliath was raised. See the G on his letter jacket? Gath High School. His ancestors were to Hebrews what pirates were to Her Majesty's navy.

Saul's soldiers saw Goliath and mumbled, "Not again. My dad fought his dad. My granddad fought his granddad."

You've groaned similar words. "I'm becoming a workaholic, just like my father." "Divorce streaks through our family tree like oak wilt." "My mom couldn't keep a friend either. Is this ever going to stop?"

Goliath: the long-standing bully of the valley. Tougher than a two-dollar steak. More snarls than twin Dobermans. He awaits you in the morning, torments you at night. He stalked your ancestors and now looms over you. He blocks the sun and leaves you standing in the shadow of a doubt. "When Saul and his troops heard the Philistine's challenge, they were terrified and lost all hope" (17:11 MSG).

But what am I telling you? You know Goliath. You recognize his walk and wince at his talk. You've seen your Godzilla. The question is, is he all you see? You know his voice—but is it all you hear? David saw and heard more. Read the first words he spoke, not just in the battle, but in the Bible: "David asked the men standing near him, 'What will be done for the man who kills this Philistine and removes this disgrace from Israel? Who is this uncircumcised Philistine that he should defy the armies of the living God?'" (17:26 NIV).

David shows up discussing God. The soldiers mentioned nothing about him, the brothers never spoke his name, but David takes one step onto the stage and raises the subject of the living God. He does the same with King Saul: no chitchat about the battle or questions about the odds. Just a God-birthed announcement: "The Lord, who delivered me from the paw of the lion and from the paw of the bear, He will deliver me from the hand of this Philistine" (17:37 NKJV).

He continues the theme with Goliath. When the giant mocks David, the shepherd boy replies:

"You come against me with sword and spear and javelin, but I come against you in the name of the Lord Almighty, the God of the armies of Israel, whom you have defied. This day the Lord will hand you over to me, and I'll strike you down and cut off your head. Today I will give the carcasses of the Philistine army to the birds of the air and the beasts of the earth, and the whole world will know that there is a God in Israel. All those gathered here will know that it is not by sword or spear that the Lord saves; for the battle is the Lord's, and he will give all of you into our hands." (17:45–47 NIV)

No one else discusses God. David discusses no one else but God.

A subplot appears in the story. More than "David versus Goliath," this is "God-focus versus giant-focus."

David sees what others don't and refuses to see what others do. All eyes, except David's, fall on the brutal, hate-breathing hulk. All compasses, sans David's, are set on the polestar of the Philistine. All journals, but David's, describe day after day in the land of the Neanderthal. The people know his taunts, demands, size, and strut. They have majored in Goliath.

David majors in God. He sees the giant, mind you; he just sees God more so. Look carefully at David's battle cry: "You come to me with a sword, with a spear, and with a javelin. But I come to you in the name of the Lord of hosts, the God of the armies of Israel" (17:45 NKJV).

Note the plural noun—*armies* of Israel. Armies? The common observer sees only one army of Israel. Not David. He sees the Allies on D-day: platoons of angels and infantries of saints, the weapons of the wind and the forces of the earth. God could pellet the enemy with hail as he did for Moses, collapse walls as he did for Joshua, stir thunder as he did for Samuel.[2]

David sees the armies of God. And because he does, David hurries and runs toward the army to meet the Philistine (17:48).[3]

David's brothers cover their eyes, both in fear and embarrassment. Saul sighs as the young Hebrew races to certain death. Goliath throws back his head in laughter, just enough to shift his helmet and expose a square inch of forehead flesh. David spots the target and seizes the moment. The sound of the swirling sling is the only sound in the valley. Ssshhhww. Ssshhhww. Ssshhhww. The stone torpedoes through the air and into the skull; Goliath's eyes cross and legs buckle. He crumples to the ground and dies. David runs over and yanks Goliath's sword from its sheath, shish-kebabs the Philistine, and cuts off his head.

You might say that David knew how to get *a head* of his giant.

When was the last time you did the same? How long since you ran toward your challenge? We tend to retreat, duck behind a desk of work or crawl into a nightclub of distraction or a bed of forbidden love. For a moment, a day, or a year, we feel safe, insulated, anesthetized, but then the work runs out, the liquor wears off, or the lover leaves, and we hear Goliath again. Booming. Bombastic.

Try a different tack. Rush your giant with a God-saturated soul. *Giant of divorce, you aren't entering my home! Giant of depression? It may take a lifetime, but you won't conquer me. Giant of alcohol, bigotry, child abuse, insecurity . . . you're going down.* How long since you loaded your sling and took a swing at your giant?

Too long, you say? Then David is your model. God called him "a man after my own heart" (Acts 13:22 NIV). He gave the appellation to no one else. Not Abraham or Moses or Joseph. He called Paul an apostle, John his beloved, but neither was tagged a man after God's own heart.

One might read David's story and wonder what God saw in him. The fellow fell as often as he stood, stumbled as often as he conquered. He stared down Goliath, yet ogled at Bathsheba; defied God-mockers in the valley, yet joined them in the wilderness. An Eagle Scout one day. Chumming with the Mafia the next. He could lead armies but couldn't manage a family. Raging David. Weeping David. Bloodthirsty. God-hungry. Eight wives. One God.

A man after God's own heart? That God saw him as such gives hope to us all. David's life has little to offer the unstained saint. Straight-A souls find David's story disappointing. The rest of us find it reassuring. We ride the same roller coaster. We alternate between swan dives and belly flops, soufflés and burnt toast.

In David's good moments, no one was better. In his bad moments, could one be worse? The heart God loved was a checkered one.

We need David's story. Giants lurk in our neighborhoods. Rejection. Failure. Revenge. Remorse. Our struggles read like a prizefighter's itinerary:

- "In the main event, we have Joe the Decent Guy versus the fraternity from *Animal House*."
- "Weighing in at 110 pounds, Elizabeth the Checkout Girl will go toe to toe with Jerks who Take and Break Her Heart."
- "In this corner, the tenuous marriage of Jason and Patricia. In the opposing corner, the challenger from the state of confusion, the home breaker named Distrust."

Giants. We must face them. Yet we need not face them alone. Focus first, and most, on God. The times David did, giants fell. The days he didn't, David did.

Test this theory with an open Bible. Read 1 Samuel 17 and list the observations David made regarding Goliath.

I find only two. One statement to Saul about Goliath (v. 36). And one to Goliath's face: "Who is this uncircumcised Philistine that he should defy the armies of the living God?" (v. 26 NIV).

That's it. Two Goliath-related comments (and tacky ones at that) and no questions. No inquiries about Goliath's skill, age, social standing, or IQ. David asks nothing about the weight of the spear, the size of the shield, or the meaning of the skull and crossbones tattooed on the giant's bicep. David gives no thought to the diplodocus on the hill. Zilch.

But he gives much thought to God. Read David's words again, this time underlining his references to his Lord.

"The armies of *the living God*" (v. 26).

"The armies of *the living God*" (v. 36).

"*The* LORD of hosts, the God of the armies of Israel" (v. 45 NKJV).

"*The* LORD will deliver you into my hand . . . that all the earth may know that *there is a God* in Israel" (v. 46 NKJV).

"*The* L*ord* does not save with sword and spear; for *the battle is the Lord's, and He will give you into our hands*" (v. 47 NKJV).[4]

I count nine references. God-thoughts outnumber Goliath-thoughts nine to two. How does this ratio compare with yours? Do you ponder God's grace four times as much as you ponder your guilt? Is your list of blessings four times as long as your list of complaints? Is your mental file of hope four times as thick as your mental file of dread? Are you four times as likely to describe the strength of God as you are the demands of your day?

No? Then David is your man.

Some note the absence of miracles in his story. No Red Sea openings, chariots flaming, or dead Lazaruses walking. No miracles.

But there is one. David is one. A rough-edged walking wonder of God who neon-lights this truth:

Focus on giants—you stumble.

Focus on God—your giants tumble.

Lift your eyes, giant-slayer. The God who made a miracle out of David stands ready to make one out of you.

For Reflection and Discussion

1. What Goliaths have you confronted in the past? How does your Goliath block your vision of God and make it harder to hear from the Lord?

2. "David majors in God. He sees the giant, mind you; he just sees God more so." How does majoring in God help to shrink the Goliaths of your life?

3. When you focus on your giants, what kind of stumbles do you tend to take? When you focus on God, what kind of tumbles do your giants tend to take?

4. Read 1 Samuel 17:1–54. What reason does David give for his confidence in a fight against Goliath (vv. 34–37)? What do verses 45–47 reveal about the man after God's own heart?

5. What Goliath is staring you in the face right now, taunting you and defying God to rescue you? Set aside an hour in which you focus on God—on his power and his wisdom and his glory—and in which you concentrate your prayers for help on this problem. Watch God make a fast turning point in this battle!

Chapter 15

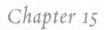

ESTHER

Then Mordecai sent back word to Esther: "Just because you live in the king's palace, don't think that out of all the Jewish people you alone will escape. If you keep quiet at this time, someone else will help and save the Jewish people, but you and your father's family will all die. And who knows, you may have been chosen queen for just such a time as this."

Then Esther sent this answer to Mordecai: "Go and get all the Jewish people in Susa together. For my sake, fast; do not eat or drink for three days, night and day. I and my servant girls will also fast . Then I will go to the king, even though it is against the law, and if I die, I die.". . .

The king asked Esther again, "What are you asking for? I will give it to you. What is it you want? I will give you as much as half of my kingdom."

Then Queen Esther answered, "My king, if you are pleased with me, and if it pleases you, let me live. This is what I ask. And let my people live, too. This is what I want."

{ EST. 4:13–16; 7:2–3 }

TOUCHING THE KING'S HEART

O ur family went desk hunting recently. I needed a new one for the office, and we'd promised Andrea and Sara desks for their rooms. Sara was especially enthused. When she comes home from school, guess what she does? She plays school! I never did that as a kid. I tried to forget the classroom activities, not rehearse them. Denalyn assures me not to worry, that this is one of those attention-span differences between genders. So off to the furniture store we went.

When Denalyn buys furniture she prefers one of two extremes—so antique it's fragile or so new it's unpainted. This time we opted for the latter and entered a store of in-the-buff furniture.

Andrea and Sara succeeded quickly in making their selections, and I set out to do the same. Somewhere in the process Sara learned we weren't taking the desks home that day, and this news disturbed her deeply. I explained that the piece had to be painted and they would deliver the desk in about four weeks. I might as well have said four millennia.

Her eyes filled with tears, "But, Daddy, I wanted to take it home today."

Much to her credit she didn't stomp her feet and demand her way. She did, however, set out on an urgent course to change her father's mind. Every time I turned a corner she was waiting on me.

"Daddy, don't you think we could paint it ourselves?"

"Daddy, I just want to draw some pictures on my new desk."

"Daddy, please let's take it home today."

After a bit she disappeared, only to return, arms open wide and bubbling with a discovery. "Guess what, Daddy. It'll fit in the back of the car!"

You and I know that a seven-year-old has no clue what will or won't fit in a vehicle, but the fact that she had measured the trunk with her arms softened my heart. The clincher, though, was the name she called me: "Daddy, can't we please take it home?"

The Lucado family took a desk home that day.

I heard Sara's request for the same reason God hears ours. Her desire was for her own good. What dad wouldn't want his child to spend more time writing and drawing? Sara wanted what I wanted for her, she only wanted it sooner. When we agree with what God wants, he hears us, as well (see 1 John 5:14).

Sara's request was heartfelt. God, too, is moved by our sincerity. The "earnest prayer of a righteous man has great power" (James 5:16 TLB).

But most of all, I was moved to respond because Sara called me "Daddy." Because she is my child, I heard her request. Because we are his children, God hears ours. The king of creation gives special heed to the voice of his family. He is not only willing to hear us, he loves to hear us. He even tells us what to ask him.

"Thy kingdom come."

THY KINGDOM COME

We're often content to ask for less. We enter the throne room of God with a satchel full of requests—promotions desired, pay raises wanted, transmission repairs needed, and tuitions due. We'd typically say our prayers as casually as we'd order a burger at the drive-through: "I'll have one solved problem and two blessings, cut the hassles, please."

But such complacency seems inappropriate in the chapel of worship. Here we are before the King of kings. The pay raise is still needed and the promotion is still desired, but is that where we start?

Jesus tells how to begin. "When you pray, pray like this. 'Our Father who is in heaven, hallowed be thy name. Thy kingdom come.'"

When you say, "Thy kingdom come," you are inviting the Messiah himself to walk into your world. "Come, my King! Take your throne in our land. Be present in my heart. Be present in my office. Come into my marriage. Be Lord of my family, my fears, and my doubts." This is no feeble request; it's a bold appeal for God to occupy every corner of your life.

Who are you to ask such a thing? Who are you to ask God to take control of your world? You are his child, for heaven's sake! And so you ask boldly. "So let us come boldly to the very throne of God and stay there to receive his mercy and to find grace to help us in our times of need" (Heb. 4:16).

A Spiritual Drama

A wonderful illustration of this kind of boldness is in the story of Hadassah. Though her language and culture are an atlas apart from ours, she can tell you about the power of a prayer to a king. There are a couple of differences, though. Her request was not to her father, but to her husband, the king. Her prayer wasn't for a desk, but for the delivery of her people. And because she entered the throne room, because she opened her heart to the king, he changed his plans and millions of people in 127 different countries were saved.

Oh, how I'd love for you to meet Hadassah. But since she lived in the fifth century BC, such an encounter is not likely. We'll have to be content with reading about her in the book which bears her name—her other name—the book of Esther.

And what a book it is! Hollywood would have a challenge matching the drama of this story . . . the evil Haman who demanded that all pay him homage . . . the gutsy Mordecai who refused to bow before Haman . . . Mordecai's great words to Esther that she may have been chosen queen for "such a time as this" . . . and Esther's conviction to save her people. "If I perish, I perish," she resolved.

Let's review the central characters.

Xerxes was the king of Persia. He was an absolute monarch over the land from India to Ethiopia. Let Xerxes raise an eyebrow and the destiny of the world would change. In this respect he symbolized the power of God, for our King guides the river of life, and he doesn't even raise an eyebrow.

Haman (whose name sounds like hangman, which you will soon see as more than a curious coincidence) was the right-hand man of Xerxes. Read every word about the man and you'll find nothing good about him. He was an insatiable egotist who wanted the worship of every person in the kingdom. Perturbed by a peculiar minority called the Jews, he decided to exterminate them. He convinced Xerxes that the world would be better with a holocaust and set a date for the genocide of all of Abraham's children.

Haman is a servant of hell and a picture of the devil himself, who has no higher aim than to have every knee bow as he passes. Satan also has no other plan than to persecute the promised people of God. He comes to "steal and kill and destroy" (John 10:10). "He is filled with anger, because he knows he does not have much time" (Rev. 12:12). Since the lie in the garden, he has sought to derail God's plan. In this case Satan hopes to destroy the Jews, thereby destroying the lineage of Jesus. For Haman, the massacre is a matter of expediency. For Satan, it is a matter of survival. He will do whatever it takes to impede the presence of Jesus in the world.

That's why he doesn't want you to pray as Jesus taught, "Thy kingdom come."

Esther, Mordecai's adopted daughter, became queen by winning a Miss Persia contest. In one day she went from obscurity to royalty, and in more ways than one she reminds you of you. Both of you are residents of the palace: Esther, the bride of Xerxes and you, the bride of Christ. Both of you have access to the throne of the king, and you both have a counselor to guide and teach you. Your counselor is the Holy Spirit. Esther's counselor was Mordecai.

It was Mordecai who urged Esther to keep her Jewish nationality a secret. It was also Mordecai who persuaded Esther to talk to Xerxes about the impending massacre. You may wonder why she would need any encouragement. Mordecai must have wondered the same thing. Listen to the message he got from Esther:

> "No man or woman may go to the king in the inner courtyard without being called. There is only one law about this: Anyone who enters must be put to death unless the king holds out his gold scepter. Then that person may live. And I have not been called to go to the king for thirty days." (Est. 4:11)

As strange as it may sound to us, not even the queen could approach the king without an invitation. To enter his throne room uninvited was to risk a visit to the gallows. But Mordecai convinces her to take the risk. If you wonder why I see Mordecai as a picture of the Holy Spirit, watch how he encourages her to do what is right. "Just because you think you live in the king's palace, don't think that out of all the Jewish people you alone will escape. If you keep quiet at this time, someone else will help and save the Jewish people, but you and your father's family will all die. And who knows, you may have been chosen queen for such a time as this" (Est. 4:13–14).

Watch how Esther responds. "Esther put on her royal robes and stood in the inner courtyard of the king's palace, facing the king's hall" (Est. 5:1).

Can't you see her? Right off the cover of *Mademoiselle* magazine? Can't you see King Xerxes? Flipping through his copy of *Car and Chariot*. On either side of him is a burly-chested guard. Behind him is a chattering eunuch. Ahead of him is a long day of cabinet meetings and royal red tape. He lets out a sigh and sinks down into his throne . . . and out of the corner of his eye, he sees Esther.

"When the king saw Queen Esther standing in the courtyard, he was pleased" (5:2). Let me give you my translation of that verse: "When the king saw Queen Esther standing in the courtyard he said, 'a-hubba-

hubba-hubba.'" "He held out to her the gold scepter that was in his hand, so Esther went forward and touched the end of it" (5:2).

What follows is the rapid collapse of Satan's deck of cards. Haman schemes to string up Mordecai, the only man who won't grovel at his feet. Esther plans to throw a couple of banquets for Xerxes and Haman. At the end of the second banquet Xerxes begs Esther to ask for something. Esther looks sort of sheepishly at the floor and says, "Well, now that you mention it, there is one eensy weensy favor I've been wanting to ask." And she proceeds to inform the king about the raging anti-Semite who was hell-bent on killing her friends like rats, which meant that Xerxes was about to lose his bride if he didn't act soon, and you don't want that, do you honey?

Xerxes demands the name of the murderer, and Haman looks for the exits. Esther spills the beans, and Xerxes loses his cool. He storms out the door to take a Prozac only to return and find Haman at the feet of Esther. Haman is begging for mercy, but the king thinks he's making a move on the queen. And before Haman has a chance to explain, he's headed to the same gallows he'd built for Mordecai.

Haman gets Mordecai's rope. Mordecai gets Haman's job. Esther gets a good night's sleep. The Jews live to see another day. And we get a dramatic reminder of what happens when we approach our King.

Like Esther, we have been plucked out of obscurity and given a place in the palace.

Like Esther, we have royal robes; she was dressed in cloth, we are dressed in righteousness.

Like Esther, we have the privilege of making our request.

That's what Sara did. Her request wasn't as dramatic as Esther's, but it changed her father's plans. By the way, the living parable of Sara and her desk didn't stop at the store.

On the way home she realized that my desk was still at the store. "I guess you didn't beg, did you, Daddy?" (We have not because we ask not.)

When we unloaded her desk she invited me to christen it with her by drawing a picture. I made a sign which read, "Sara's desk." She made a sign which read, "I love my Daddy." (Worship is the right response to answered prayer.)

My favorite part of the story is what happened the next day. I shared this account in my Sunday sermon. A couple from our church dropped by and picked the desk up, telling us they would paint it. When they returned it a couple of days later, it was covered with angels. And I was reminded that when we pray for God's kingdom to come, it comes! All the hosts of heaven rush to our aid.

FOR REFLECTION AND DISCUSSION

1. Consider the phrase "thy kingdom come." When you think of God's coming kingdom, what comes to mind? Why do you think we should pray that God's kingdom would come?
2. Read Esther 3–9. What part did Esther play in this drama? What part did Mordecai play? What was the role of the king? From the text's point of view, who is the central character?
3. If God's kingdom were to come into your workplace, what would happen? In your marriage? In your family?
4. Read Hebrews 4:14–16. What conclusion is made in verse 16, based on what is said in verses 14–15? Do you take advantage of this promise? Why or why not?
5. Spend some time asking God to occupy every corner of your life. What "corners" might you still be withholding from him? Finances? Relationships? Work? School? Recreation? Be as honest with yourself as possible and take inventory of your life. Then invite the King to take control in every area.

JOB

A man named Job lived in the land of Uz. He was an honest and innocent man; he honored God and stayed away from evil. Job had seven sons and three daughters. He owned seven thousand sheep, three thousand camels, five hundred teams of oxen, and five hundred female donkeys. He also had a large number of servants. He was the greatest man among all the people of the East.

The LORD said to Satan, "All right, then. Job is in your power, but you may not take his life."

So Satan left the LORD's presence. He put painful sores on Job's body, from the top of his head to the soles of his feet. Job took a piece of broken pottery to scrape himself, and he sat in ashes in misery.

The LORD said to Job:

"Will the person who argues with the Almighty correct him?
Let the person who accuses God answer him."

Then Job answered the LORD:

"I am not worthy; I cannot answer you anything,
so I will put my hand over my mouth."

{ JOB 1:1–3; 2:6–8; 40:1–4 }

WHERE MAN COVERS
HIS MOUTH

When I lived in Brazil I took my mom and her friend to see Iguacu Falls, the largest waterfalls in the world. Some weeks earlier I'd become an expert on the cataracts by reading an article in *National Geographic* magazine. Surely, I thought, my guests would appreciate their good fortune in having me as a guide.

To reach the lookout point, tourists must walk a winding trail that leads them through a forest. I took advantage of the hike to give an Iguacu nature report to my mom and her friend. So full of information I was, I chattered the entire time. After some minutes, however, I caught myself speaking louder and louder. A sound in the distance forced me to raise my voice. With each turn in the trail, my volume increased. Finally, I was shouting above a roar which was proving to be quite irritating. *Whatever that noise is, I wish they'd shut it off so I could complete my lecture.*

Only after reaching the clearing did I realize that the noise we heard was the waterfalls. My words were drowned out by the force and fury of what I was trying to describe. I could no longer be heard. Even if I could, I no longer had an audience. Even my mother would rather see the splendor than hear my description. I shut my mouth.

There are times when to speak is to violate the moment . . . when silence represents the highest respect. The word for such times is reverence. The prayer for such times is "Hallowed be thy name." Only you and God are here, and you can surmise who occupies the throne.

Don't worry about having the right words; worry more about having the right heart. It's not eloquence he seeks, just honesty.

A TIME TO BE SILENT

This was a lesson Job learned. If he had a fault, it was his tongue. He talked too much.

Not that anyone could blame him. Calamity had pounced on the man like a lioness on a herd of gazelles, and by the time the rampage passed, there was hardly a wall standing or a loved one living. Enemies had slaughtered Job's cattle, and lightning had destroyed his sheep. Strong winds had left his partying kids buried in wreckage.

And that was just the first day.

Job hadn't even had time to call Allstate before he saw the leprosy on his hands and the boils on his skin. His wife, compassionate soul that she was, told him to "curse God and die." His four friends came with the bedside manner of drill sergeants, telling him that God is fair and pain is the result of evil, and as sure as two-plus-two equals four, Job must have some criminal record in his past to suffer so.

Each had his own interpretation of God and each spoke long and loud about who God is and why God did what he did. They weren't the only ones talking about God. When his accusers paused, Job gave his response. Back and forth they went . . .

> Job cried out . . . (3:1).
> Then Eliphaz the Temanite answered . . . (4:1).
> Then Job answered . . . (6:1).
> Then Bildad the Shuhite answered . . . (8:1).
> Then Job answered . . . (9:1).
> Then Zophath the Naamathite answered . . . (11:1).

This verbal ping-pong continues for twenty-three chapters. Finally Job has enough of this "answering." No more discussion-group chitchat. It's time for the keynote address. He grips the microphone with one hand and the pulpit with the other and launches forth. For six chapters Job gives his opinions on God. This time the chapter headings read: "And Job continued," "And Job continued," "And Job continued." He defines God, explains God, and reviews God. One gets the impression that Job knows more about God than God does!

We are thirty-seven chapters into the book before God clears his throat to speak. Chapter thirty-eight begins with these words: "Then the LORD answered Job."

If your Bible is like mine, there is a mistake in this verse. The words are fine but the printer uses the wrong size type. The words should look like this:

THEN THE LORD ANSWERED JOB!

God speaks. Faces turn toward the sky. Winds bend the trees. Neighbors plunge into the storm shelters. Cats scurry up the trees and dogs duck into the bushes. "Somethin's a-blowin' in, honey. Best get them sheets off the line." God has no more than opened his mouth before Job knows he should have kept his sore one shut.

"I will ask you questions and you must answer me. Where were you when I made the earth's foundation? Tell me if you understand. Who marked off how big it should be? Surely you know! Who stretched a ruler across it? What were the earth's foundations set on, or who put its cornerstone in place while the morning stars sang together and all the angels shouted with joy?" (38:3–6)

God floods the sky with queries, and Job cannot help but get the point: Only God defines God. You've got to know the alphabet before you can read, and God tells Job, "You don't even know the ABC's of heaven, much less the vocabulary." For the first time, Job is quiet. Silenced by a torrent of questions.

Have you ever gone to where the sea begins or walked the valleys under the sea? . . . Have you ever gone to the storehouse for snow or seen the storehouses for hail . . . ? Are you the one who gives the horse his strength or puts the flowing mane on its neck? Do you make the horse jump like a locust? Is it through your wisdom that the hawk flies and spreads its wings toward the south? (38:16, 22; 39:19–20, 26)

Job barely has time to shake his head at one question before he is asked another. The Father's implication is clear: "As soon as you are able to handle these simple matters of storing stars and stretching the neck of the ostrich, then we'll have a talk about pain and suffering. But until then, we can do without your commentary."

Does Job get the message? I think so. Listen to his response. "I am not worthy; I cannot answer you anything, so I will put my hand over my mouth" (40:4).

Notice the change. Before he heard God, Job couldn't speak enough. After he heard God, he couldn't speak at all.

Silence was the only proper response. There was a time in the life of Thomas à Kempis when he, too, covered his mouth. He had written profusely about the character of God. But one day God confronted him with such holy grace that, from that moment on, all à Kempis's words "seemed like straw." He put down his pen and never wrote another line. He put his hand over his mouth.

The word for such moments is reverence: "Hallowed be thy name."

A CUT ABOVE

This phrase is a petition, not a proclamation. A request, not an announcement. Hallowed *be* your name. Do whatever it takes to be holy in my life. Take your rightful place on the throne. Exalt yourself. Magnify yourself. Glorify yourself. You be Lord, and I'll be quiet.

The word *hallowed* comes from the word *holy*, and the word *holy* means "to separate." The ancestry of the term can be traced back to an ancient word which means "to cut." To be holy, then, is to be a cut above the norm, superior, extraordinary. The Holy One dwells on a different level from the rest of us. What frightens us does not frighten him. What troubles us does not trouble him.

I'm more a landlubber than a sailor, but I've puttered around in a bass boat enough to know the secret for finding land in a storm . . . You don't aim at another boat. You certainly don't stare at the waves. You set your sights on an object unaffected by the wind—a light on the shore—and go straight toward it. The light is unaffected by the storm.

When you set your sights on our God, you focus on one "a cut above" any storm life may bring.

Like Job, you find peace in the pain.

Like Job, you cover your mouth and sit still.

"Be still and know that I am God" (Ps. 46:10). This verse contains a command with a promise.

The command?

Be still.

Cover your mouth.

Bend your knees.

The promise? You will *know that I am God.*

The vessel of faith journeys on soft waters. Belief rides on the wings of waiting.

In the midst of your daily storms, make it a point to be still and set your sights on him. Let God be God. Let him bathe you in his glory so that both your breath and your troubles are sucked from your soul. Be still. Be quiet. Be open and willing. Then you will know that God is God, and you can't help but confess, "Hallowed be thy name."

FOR REFLECTION AND DISCUSSION

1. How does one "hallow" God's name? From the opposite viewpoint, how does one profane it? In the last week, did you do more of one than the other? Explain.
2. Read Job 38:3–18. What is the point of all of God's questions? What lesson does he want Job to learn? What do you learn about God in this passage?
3. Read Job 40:4–5; 42:1–6. What did Job finally learn about God? How did it change his attitude toward his circumstances?
4. If you had been in Job's shoes, do you think you would have reacted much as he did? Why or why not?
5. In times of trouble, do you ever demand answers of God? If he were to respond to your questions, what do you think he'd say?

Chapter 17

NICODEMUS

There was a man of the Pharisees named Nicodemus, a ruler of the Jews. This man came to Jesus by night and said to Him, "Rabbi, we know that You are a teacher come from God; for no one can do these signs that You do unless God is with him."

Jesus answered and said to him, "Most assuredly, I say to you, unless one is born again, he cannot see the kingdom of God."

Nicodemus said to Him, "How can a man be born when he is old? Can he enter a second time into his mother's womb and be born?"

Jesus answered, "Most assuredly, I say to you, unless one is born of water and the Spirit, he cannot enter the kingdom of God. That which is born of the flesh is flesh, and that which is born of the Spirit is spirit. Do not marvel that I said to you, 'You must be born again.' The wind blows where it wishes, and you hear the sound of it, but cannot tell where it comes from and where it goes. So is everyone who is born of the Spirit."

Nicodemus answered and said to Him, "How can these things be?" Jesus answered and said to him, "Are you the teacher of Israel, and do not know these things? Most assuredly, I say to you, We speak what We know and testify what We have seen, and you do not receive Our witness. If I have told you earthly things and you do not believe, how will you believe if I tell you heavenly things? No one has ascended to heaven but He who came down from heaven, that is, the Son of Man who is in heaven. And as Moses lifted up the serpent in the wilderness, even so must the Son of Man be lifted up, that whoever believes in Him should not perish but have eternal life. For God so loved the world that He gave His only begotten Son, that whoever believes in Him should not perish but have everlasting life. For God did not send His Son into the world to condemn the world, but that the world through Him might be saved."

{ JOHN 3:1–17 NKJV }

The Most Famous
Conversation
in the Bible

He's waiting for the shadows. Darkness will afford the cover he covets. So he waits for the safety of nightfall. He sits near the second-floor window of his house, sipping olive-leaf tea, watching the sunset, biding his time. Jerusalem enchants at this hour. The disappearing sunlight tints the stone streets, gilds the white houses, and highlights the blockish temple.

Nicodemus looks across the slate roofs at the massive square: gleaming and resplendent. He walked its courtyard this morning. He'll do so again tomorrow. He'll gather with religious leaders and do what religious leaders do: discuss God. Discuss reaching God, pleasing God, appeasing God.

God.

Pharisees converse about God. And Nicodemus sits among them. Debating. Pondering. Solving puzzles. Resolving dilemmas. *Sandal-tying on the Sabbath. Feeding people who won't work. Divorcing your wife. Dishonoring parents.*

What does God say? Nicodemus needs to know. It's his job. He's a holy man and leads holy men. His name appears on the elite list of Torah scholars. He dedicated his life to the law and occupies one of the seventy-one seats of the Judean supreme court. He has credentials, clout, and questions.

Questions for this Galilean crowd-stopper. This backwater teacher who lacks diplomas yet attracts people. Who has ample time for the happy-hour crowd but little time for clergy and the holy upper crust. He banishes demons, some say; forgives sin, others claim; purifies temples,

Nicodemus has no doubt. He witnessed Jesus purge Solomon's Porch.[1] He saw the fury. Braided whip, flying doves. "There will be no pocket padding in my house!" Jesus erupted. By the time the dust settled and coins landed, hustling clerics were running a background check on him. The man from Nazareth won no favor in the temple that day.

So Nicodemus comes at night. His colleagues can't know of the meeting. They wouldn't understand. But Nicodemus can't wait until they do. As the shadows darken the city, he steps out, slips unseen through the cobbled, winding streets. He passes servants lighting lamps in the courtyards and takes a path that ends at the door of a simple house. Jesus and his followers are staying here, he's been told. Nicodemus knocks.

The noisy room silences as he enters. The men are wharf workers and tax collectors, unaccustomed to the highbrow world of a scholar. They shift in their seats. Jesus motions for the guest to sit. Nicodemus does and initiates the most famous conversation in the Bible: "Rabbi, we know that You are a teacher come from God; for no one can do these signs that You do unless God is with him" (John 3:2 NKJV).

Nicodemus begins with what he "knows." *I've done my homework*, he implies. *Your work impresses me.*

We listen for a kindred salutation from Jesus: "And I've heard of you, Nicodemus." We expect, and Nicodemus expected, some hospitable chitchat.

None comes. Jesus makes no mention of Nicodemus's VIP status, good intentions, or academic credentials, not because they don't exist, but because, in Jesus' algorithm, they don't matter. He simply issues this proclamation: "Unless one is born again, he cannot see the kingdom of God" (v. 3 NKJV).

Behold the Continental Divide of Scripture, the international date line of faith. Nicodemus stands on one side, Jesus on the other, and Christ pulls no punches about their differences.

Nicodemus inhabits a land of good efforts, sincere gestures, and hard work. Give God your best, his philosophy says, and God does the rest.

Jesus' response? Your best won't do. Your works don't work. Your finest efforts don't mean squat. Unless you are born again, you can't even see what God is up to.

Nicodemus hesitates on behalf of us all. Born again? "How can a man be born when he is old?" (v. 4 NKJV). You must be kidding. Put life in reverse? Rewind the tape? Start all over? We can't be born again.

Oh, but wouldn't we like to? A do-over. A try-again. A reload. Broken hearts and missed opportunities bob in our wake. A mulligan would be nice. Who wouldn't cherish a second shot? But who can pull it off? Nicodemus scratches his chin and chuckles. "Yeah, a graybeard like me gets a maternity-ward recall."

Jesus doesn't crack a smile. "Most assuredly, I say to you, unless one is born of water and the Spirit, he cannot enter the kingdom of God" (v. 5 NKJV). About this time a gust of wind blows a few leaves through the still-open door. Jesus picks one off the floor and holds it up. God's power works like that wind, Jesus explains. Newborn hearts are born of heaven. You can't wish, earn, or create one. New birth? Inconceivable. God handles the task, start to finish.

Nicodemus looks around the room at the followers. Their blank expressions betray equal bewilderment.

Old Nick has no hook upon which to hang such thoughts. He speaks self-fix. But Jesus speaks—indeed introduces—a different language. Not works born of men and women, but a work done by God.

Born again. Birth, by definition, is a passive act. The enwombed child contributes nothing to the delivery. Postpartum celebrations applaud the work of the mother. No one lionizes the infant. ("Great work there, little one.") No, give the tyke a pacifier not a medal. Mom deserves the gold. She exerts the effort. She pushes, agonizes, and delivers.

When my niece bore her first child, she invited her brother and mother to stand in the delivery room. After witnessing three hours of pushing, when the baby finally crowned, my nephew turned to his mom and said, "I'm sorry for every time I talked back to you."

The mother pays the price of birth. She doesn't enlist the child's assistance or solicit his or her advice. Why would she? The baby can't even take a breath without umbilical help, much less navigate a path into new life. Nor, Jesus is saying, can we. Spiritual rebirthing requires a capable parent, not an able infant.

Who is this parent? Check the strategically selected word *again*. The Greek language offers two choices for *again*:[2]

1. *Palin*, which means a repetition of an act; to redo what was done earlier.[3]
2. *Anothen*, which also depicts a repeated action, but requires the original source to repeat it. It means "from above, from a higher place, things which come from heaven or God."[4] In other words, the one who did the work the first time does it again. This is the word Jesus chose.

The difference between the two terms is the difference between a painting by da Vinci and one by me. Suppose you and I are standing in the Louvre, admiring the famous *Mona Lisa*. Inspired by the work, I produce an easel and canvas and announce, "I'm going to paint this beautiful portrait again."

And I do! Right there in the Salle des Etats, I brandish my palette and flurry my brush and re-create the *Mona Lisa*. Alas, Lucado is no Leonardo. Ms. Lisa has a Picassoesque imbalance to her—crooked nose and one eye higher than the other. Technically, however, I keep my pledge and paint the *Mona Lisa again*.

Jesus means something else. He employs the second Greek term, calling for the action of the original source. He uses the word *anothen*, which, if honored in the Paris gallery, would require da Vinci's presence. *Anothen* excludes:

Latter-day replicas.

Second-generation attempts.

Well-meaning imitations.

He who did it first must do it again. The original creator recreates his creation. This is the act that Jesus describes.

Born: God exerts the effort.

Again: God restores the beauty.

We don't try again. We need, not the muscle of self, but a miracle of God.

The thought coldcocks Nicodemus. "How can this be?" (v. 9). Jesus answers by leading him to the Hope diamond of the Bible.

> For God
> so loved the world
> that he gave his one and only Son,
> that whoever believes in him
> shall not perish but have
> eternal life.

A twenty-six-word parade of hope: beginning with God, ending with life, and urging us to do the same. Brief enough to write on a napkin or memorize in a moment, yet solid enough to weather two thousand years of storms and questions. If you know nothing of the Bible, start here. If you know everything in the Bible, return here. We all need the reminder. The heart of the human problem is the heart of the human. And God's treatment is prescribed in John 3:16.

He loves.

He gave.

We believe.

We live.

The words are to Scripture what the Mississippi River is to America—an entryway into the heartland. Believe or dismiss them, embrace or reject them, any serious consideration of Christ must include them. Would a British historian dismiss the Magna Carta? Egyptologists overlook the

Rosetta stone? Could you ponder the words of Christ and never immerse yourself into John 3:16?

The verse is an alphabet of grace, a table of contents to the Christian hope, each word a safe-deposit box of jewels. Read it again, slowly and aloud, and note the word that snatches your attention. "For God so loved the world that he gave his one and only Son, that whoever believes in him shall not perish but have eternal life."

"God so *loved* the world . . ." We'd expect an anger-fueled God. One who punishes the world, recycles the world, forsakes the world . . . but loves the world?

The *world*? This world? Heartbreakers, hope-snatchers, and dream-dousers prowl this orb. Dictators rage. Abusers inflict. Reverends think they deserve the title. But God loves. And he loves the world so much he gave his:

Declarations?

Rules?

Dicta?

Edicts?

No. The heart-stilling, mind-bending, deal-making-or-breaking claim of John 3:16 is this: *God gave his son . . . his only son.* No abstract ideas but a flesh-wrapped divinity. Scripture equates Jesus with God. God, then, gave himself. Why? So that "*whoever* believes in him shall not perish."

John Newton, who set faith to music in "Amazing Grace," loved this barrier-breaking pronoun. He said, "If I read 'God so loved the world, that He gave His only begotten Son, that when John Newton believed he should have everlasting life,' I should say, perhaps, there is some other John Newton; but 'whosoever' means this John Newton and the other John Newton, and everybody else, whatever his name may be."[5]

Whoever . . . a universal word.

And *perish* . . . a sobering word. We'd like to dilute, if not delete, the term. Not Jesus. He pounds Do Not Enter signs on every square inch of Satan's gate and tells those hell-bent on entering to do so over his dead body. Even so, some souls insist.

In the end, some perish and some live. And what determines the differ-ence? Not works or talents, pedigrees or possessions. Nicodemus had these in hoards. The difference is determined by our belief. "Whoever *believes* in him shall not perish but have eternal life."

Bible translators in the New Hebrides islands struggled to find an appropriate verb for *believe*. This was a serious problem, as the word and the concept are essential to Scripture.

One Bible translator, John G. Paton, accidentally came upon a solution while hunting with a tribesman. The two men bagged a large deer and carried it on a pole along a steep mountain path to Paton's home. When they reached the veranda, both men dropped the load and plopped into the porch chairs. As they did so, the native exclaimed in the language of his people, "My, it is good to stretch yourself out here and rest." Paton immediately reached for paper and pencil and recorded the phrase.

As a result, his final translation of John 3:16 could be worded: "For God so loved the world, that he gave his only begotten Son, that whosoever stretcheth himself out on Him should not perish, but have everlasting life."[6]

Stretch out on Christ and rest.

Martin Luther did. When the great reformer was dying, severe head-aches left him bedfast and pain struck. He was offered a medication to relieve the discomfort. He declined and explained, "My best prescription for head and heart is that *God so loved the world, that He gave His only begotten Son, that whosoever believeth in Him should not perish, but have everlasting life.*"[7]

The best prescription for head and heart. Who couldn't benefit from a dose? As things turned out, Nicodemus took his share. When Jesus was crucified, the theologian showed up with Joseph of Arimathea. The two offered their respects and oversaw Jesus' burial. No small gesture, given the anti-Christ climate of the day. When word hit the streets that Jesus was out of the tomb and back on his feet, don't you know Nicodemus smiled and thought of his late-night chat?

Born again, eh? Who would've thought he'd start with himself.

For Reflection and Discussion

1. "Nicodemus inhabits a land of good efforts, sincere gestures, and hard work. Give God your best, his philosophy says, and God does the rest." Would most religious people you know affirm this philosophy? What do you think is good about it? What's wrong with it?

2. Read John 3:16 slowly and thoughtfully, as though for the first time. Which phrases strike you as the most amazing—the hardest to believe? Why?

3. "Whoever *believes* in him shall not perish but have eternal life." Is belief in Christ easy for you or difficult? Why?

4. When you approach Jesus in the night, what questions do you ask him? What answers have you received that give you comfort and hope?

5. If you have been born again, how did your life change as a result? If you have not asked Jesus into your life, consider doing it now. You can by praying this simple prayer:

Father, I believe you love this world. You gave your one and only Son so I can live forever with you. Apart from you, I die. With you, I live. I choose life. I choose you.

∝

Chapter 18

JAIRUS

A man named Jairus, a leader of the synagogue, came to Jesus and fell at his feet, begging him to come to his house. Jairus' only daughter, about twelve years old, was dying.

While Jesus was on his way to Jairus' house, the people were crowding all around him. A woman was in the crowd who had been bleeding for twelve years, but no one was able to heal her. She came up behind Jesus and touched the edge of his coat, and instantly her bleeding stopped. Then Jesus said, "Who touched me?"

When all the people said they had not touched him, Peter said, "Master, the people are all around you and are pushing against you."

But Jesus said, "Someone did touch me, because I felt power go out from me." When the woman saw she could not hide, she came forward, shaking, and fell down before Jesus. While all the people listened, she told why she had touched him and how she had been instantly healed. Jesus said to her, "Dear woman, you are made well because you believed. Go in peace."

While Jesus was still speaking, someone came from the house of the synagogue leader and said to him, "Your daughter is dead. Don't bother the teacher anymore."

When Jesus heard this, he said to Jairus, "Don't be afraid. Just believe, and your daughter will be well."

When Jesus went to the house, he let only Peter, John, James, and the girl's father and mother go inside with him. All the people were crying and feeling sad because the girl was dead, but Jesus said, "Stop crying. She is not dead, only asleep."

The people laughed at Jesus because they knew the girl was dead. But Jesus took hold of her hand and called to her, "My child, stand up!" Her spirit came back into her, and she stood up at once. Then Jesus ordered that she be given something to eat. The girl's parents were amazed, but Jesus told them not to tell anyone what had happened.

{ LUKE 8:41–56 }

THE SPARKLE FROM
ETERNITY

Wallace was an important man. He was the kind of man you would find leading a prayer at the football games or serving as president of the Lion's Club. He wore a title and a collar and had soft hands with no calluses.

He had a nice office just off the sanctuary. His secretary was a bit stale but he wasn't. He had a warm smile that melted your apprehension as you walked through his office door. He sat in a leather swivel chair and had diplomas on the wall. And he had a way of listening that made you willing to tell secrets you'd never told anyone.

He was a good man. His marriage wasn't all it could be, but it was better than most. His church was full. His name was respected. He was a fifteen-handicap golfer, and the church bought him a membership at the country club to commemorate his twentieth year with the congregation. People recognized him in public and flocked to hear him on Easter and Christmas. His retirement account was growing, and he was less than a decade from hanging up the frock and settling down to an autumn of soft wine and good books.

If he committed a sin, no one knew it. If he had a fear, no one heard it—which may have been his gravest sin.

Wallace loved people. This morning, though, he doesn't want people. He wants to be alone. He rings his secretary and advises her that he is not taking any more calls for the rest of the day. She doesn't think it unusual. He's been on the phone all morning. She thinks he needs time to study. She is partly correct. He has been on the phone all morning and he does need time. Not time to study, however. Time to weep.

Wallace looks at the eight-by-ten photo that sits on the mahogany credenza behind his desk. Through watery eyes he gazes at his twelve-year-old daughter. Braces. Pigtails. Freckles. She is a reflection of his wife—blue eyes, brown hair, pug nose. The only thing she got from her father was his heart. She owns that. And he has no intention of requesting that she return it.

She isn't his only child, but she is his last. And she is his only daughter. He'd built a fence of protection around his little girl. Maybe that is why the last few days had hurt so badly. The fence had crumbled.

It began six days ago. She came home early from school feverish and irritable. His wife put her to bed, thinking it was the flu. During the night the fever rose. The next morning they rushed her to the hospital.

The doctors were puzzled. They couldn't pinpoint the problem. They could only agree on one thing—she was sick and getting sicker.

Wallace had never known such helplessness. He didn't know how to handle his pain. He was so accustomed to being strong, he didn't know how to be weak. He assured all who called that his daughter was fine. He assured all who inquired that God was a great God. He assured everyone but himself.

Inside, his emotions were a mighty river. And his dam was beginning to crack. It was the call from the doctor this morning that broke it. "She is in a coma."

Wallace hangs up the phone and tells his secretary to hold the calls. He reaches over and takes the picture and holds it in his hands. Suddenly the words swirl in his head like a merry-go-round. "It's not fair, it's not fair."

He leans over, holds the picture to his face and weeps.

Nothing is right about it. Nothing. "Why a twelve-year-old girl? Why her, for mercy sakes?" His face hardens as he looks out his window toward the gray sky.

"Why don't you take me?" he screams.

He sits up. He walks over to the coffee table by the couch and picks up the box of tissues he keeps handy for counselees. As he's blowing his nose, he looks out the window into the courtyard of the church. An old man sits reading a paper. Another enters and sits beside him and throws bread crumbs on the cobbles. There's a rustle of wings as a covey of pigeons flutters off the roof and snatches up the food.

Don't you know my daughter is dying? How can you act as if nothing is wrong?

He's thinking about his daughter. In the springtime she used to come by every day on the way home from school. She would wait in the courtyard for him to walk her home. He would hear her chasing pigeons below and know it was time to go. He'd stop what he was doing, stand at this same window, and watch her. He'd watch her walk a tightrope on the curb around the garden. He'd watch her pick a wildflower out of the grass. He'd watch her spin around and around until she became so dizzy that she'd fall on her back and watch the clouds spin in the sky.

"Oh, Princess," he'd say. "My little girl." Then he'd stack his books and headaches on his desk and go down to meet her.

But it is not springtime and his daughter is not in the courtyard. It is winter, his little girl is nearly dead, and two old men are sitting on a bench.

"Dear, dear Princess."

Suddenly a third man enters the courtyard. He tells something to the other two. Then the three hurry out. *Must be a fight,* Wallace thinks to himself. Then he remembers. *The teacher. He is here.*

He'd almost forgotten. Jesus was arriving today. As Wallace was leaving the house this morning, his neighbor had asked him if he was going to see the controversial teacher.

Inwardly he'd scoffed at the idea. "No, too busy today," he'd answered with a wave, knowing that even on a slow day he wouldn't take time to go see an itinerant preacher. Especially this one.

The journals from headquarters had branded this guy a maverick. Some even said he was insane. But the crowds hung around him like he was God's gift to humanity.

I'm going. Wallace replayed the neighbor's response in his head.

"Yeah," Wallace had said to himself, "you also subscribe to *National Enquirer.*"

"They say he can heal . . . ," he recalled his neighbor saying.

Wallace stood up straight. Then he relaxed. "Don't be foolish."

"Faith healers are an insult to our profession," he had declared while lecturing at the seminary last fall. "Parasites of the people, charlatans of the church, prophets for profit." He'd seen these guys on television, stuffed into double-breasted suits, wearing mannequin smiles and powdered faces. He shakes his head and walks back to his desk. He picks up the photograph.

He stares at the face of the child who is about to be taken from him. "They say he can heal. . . ."

Wallace began to weigh the options. "If I go and am recognized, it will mean my job. But if she dies and he could have done something . . ." A man reaches a point where his desperation is a notch above his dignity. He shrugs his shoulders. "What choice do I have?"

The events of that afternoon redirected Wallace's life. He told the story whenever he had a chance.

I circled the bus terminal three times before I found a place to park. The cold wind bit my ears as I fumbled through my pockets looking for parking meter change. I buttoned my overcoat up to the knot of my tie, turned into the wind, and walked.

I passed a pawn shop window still flocked with Season's Greetings. Someone came out of a bar as I walked by. A dozen or so teens in skin-tight pants leaned against a brick wall. One flipped a cigarette butt at my feet. Three men in leather jackets and jeans warmed hands over a fire in a ten-gallon drum. One of them chuckled as I walked by. "Looky there, a poodle in the pound." I didn't turn around. If he was talking about me, I didn't want to know.

I felt awkward. It had been years since I'd been on this side of town. I glanced over at my reflection in a drugstore window. Wool overcoat. Wing tip shoes. Gray suit. Red tie. No wonder I was turning heads. Their question was written in their eyes. "What brings Mr. White-collar across the tracks?" The bus station was packed. I barely squeezed through the door.

Once I got in I couldn't have gotten out. Heads bobbed and ducked like corks on a lake. Everyone was trying to get across the room to the side where the de-boarded passengers entered the terminal. I managed to squeeze through ahead of them. They were just curious; I was desperate.

As I reached the window, I saw him. He stood near the bus. He had only been able to advance a couple of strides against the wall of people.

He looked too normal. He wore a corduroy jacket, the kind with patches on the elbows. His slacks weren't new, but they were nice. No tie. His hairline receded a bit before it became a flow of brown curls. I couldn't hear his voice, but I could see his face. His eyebrows were bushy. He had a gleam in his eyes and a grin on his lips—as if he were watching you unwrap the birthday present he just gave you.

He was so different from what I had anticipated I had to ask a lady next to me if that was him.

"That's him," she smiled. "That's Jesus."

He bent over and disappeared for a minute and surfaced holding a toddler. He smiled. With hands around the little boy's chest, he pushed him high into the air and held him there. The hands were rugged and slender. Someone had told me that Jesus grew up in Mississippi—the son of a mechanic in Tupelo. He brought the little boy down and began walking toward the door.

I knew if he entered the bus station, I'd never get him out. I put my hands flat against the window pane and began edging along the window. People complained but I moved anyway.

When I got to the doorway, so did Jesus. Our eyes met. I froze. I guess I hadn't considered what I would say to him. Maybe I thought he would recognize me. Maybe I thought he'd ask me if there was anything he could do. "Oh, my daughter is sick and I thought you might say a prayer . . ."

That's not how it came out. The words logjammed in my throat. I felt my eyes water, my chin quiver, and my knees hit the uneven pavement. "It's my daughter, my little girl. . . . She's very sick. Could you please touch her so she won't die?"

I regretted the words as soon as I said them. If he's a man, then I've asked the impossible. If he's more than a man, what right do I have to make such a request?

I didn't dare look up. I was ashamed. If the crowd was going anywhere, they were going to have to move around me. I didn't have the courage to raise my face.

I guess he knew I didn't. He did it for me.

I felt his fingers under my chin. He lifted my head. He didn't have to raise it far. He had knelt down in front of me. I looked into his eyes. The gaze of this young preacher embraced this old pastor like the arms of an old friend. I knew, then, that I knew this man. From somewhere I'd seen that look. I knew those eyes.

"Take me to her." His hand moved under my arm. He helped me stand. "Where is your car?"

"A car? This way!" I grabbed his hand and began to fight a path through the crowd. It wasn't easy. With my free hand I moved people like I was parting stalks of corn in a cornfield. Faces tumbled in on us. Young mothers wanting a blessing for their children. Old faces with caved-in mouths wanting release from pain.

Suddenly I lost his hand. It slipped out. I stopped and turned and saw him standing and looking. His abrupt stop surprised the crowd. They hushed. I noticed his face was pale. He spoke as if speaking to himself.

"Someone touched me."

"What?" one of his own men inquired.

"Someone touched me."

I thought he was telling a joke. He turned, slowly studying each face.

For the life of me, I couldn't tell if he was angry or delighted. He was looking for someone he didn't know but knew he'd know when he saw her.

"I touched you." The voice was beside me. Jesus pivoted.

"It was me. I'm sorry." The curtain of the crowd parted, leaving a girl on center stage. She was thin, almost frail. I could have wrapped my hand around her upper arm and touched my finger to my thumb. Her skin was dark, and her hair was in a hundred braids with beads on each end. She was coatless. She hugged her arms to herself—hands squeezing bony elbows as much out of fear as out of cold.

"Don't be afraid," Jesus assured. "What is wrong?"

"I have AIDS."

Someone behind me gasped. Several took a step back.

Jesus stepped toward her. "Tell me about it."

She looked at him, looked around at the throng of people, swallowed, and began. "I am out of money. The doctors say it is just a matter of time. I didn't have anywhere else to go. But now . . ."

She lowered her eyes and began to smile. She smiled as if someone had just whispered some good news in her ear.

I looked back at Jesus. My lands, if he wasn't smiling too! The two stood there and stared at each other, smiling like they were the only two kids in class who knew the answer to the teacher's question.

It was then I saw the look again. The same gaze met her that only moments before met me as I looked up from the pavement. Those same eyes that I knew I'd seen I saw again. Where? Where had I seen those eyes?

I turned and looked at the girl. For a moment she looked at me. I wanted to say something to her. I think she felt the same urge. We were so different, but suddenly we had everything in common: What a strange couple we were. She with her needle-tracked arms and midnight lovers; I with my clean fingernails and sermon outlines. I had spent my life telling people not to be like her. She'd spent her life avoiding hypocrites like me. But now we were thrust together against the enemy of death, desperately hoping that this country preacher could tie a knot in the end of our frazzled ropes so we could hang on.

Jesus spoke. "It was your faith that did it. Now go and enjoy life."

She resisted all effort to hide her joy. She smiled, looked back at Jesus, and jumped up and kissed him on the cheek.

The crowd laughed, Jesus blushed, and she disappeared.

I hadn't noticed, but while Jesus was speaking, some other men had worked their way into the crowd. They were standing behind me. When I heard them speak, I immediately recognized their voices. They were from my congregation.

One put his hand on my shoulder. "There's no need to bother this teacher anymore; your daughter is dead."

The words came at me like darts, but Jesus intercepted them: "Don't be afraid; just trust me."

The next few moments were a blur of activity. We raced through the crowd, jumped in the car of the man who brought the news, and sped to the hospital.

The waiting room was chaotic. Church members, neighbors, and friends were already gathering. Several wept openly. My wife, seated in one of the chairs, was pale and speechless. Her eyes were red. Her hand trembled as she brushed away a tear.

As I entered, people came to comfort me. Jesus stepped in front of them. They stopped and stared at this stranger.

"Why are you crying?" he asked. "She isn't dead; she's only asleep."

They were stunned. They were insulted. "Of all the insensitive things to say," someone shouted. "Who are you anyway?"

"Get that joker out of here!"

But leaving was the last thing Jesus had on his agenda. He turned and within a few seconds was standing in front of my daughter's hospital room. He signaled for a few of us to follow. We did.

The six of us stood at my daughter's bedside. Her face was ashen.

JAIRUS

Her lips dry and still. I touched her hand. It was cold. Before I could say anything, Jesus' hand was on mine. With the exception of one instant he never took his eyes off my daughter. But during that instant he looked at me. He looked at me with that same look, that same slight smile. He was giving another gift and couldn't wait to see the response when it was opened.

"Princess," the words were said softly, almost in a whisper, "get up!"

Her head turned slightly as if hearing a voice. Jesus stood back. Her upper body leaned forward until she was upright in bed. Her eyes opened. She turned and put her bare feet on the floor and stood.

No one moved as my wife and I watched our girl walk toward us. We held her for an eternity—half believing it couldn't be true and half not wanting to know if it wasn't. But it was.

"Better get her something to eat," Jesus teased with a smile. "She's probably famished." Then he turned to leave.

I reached out and touched his shoulder. My willingness was in my eyes. "Let me return the favor. I'll introduce you to the right people. I'll get you speaking engagements at the right places."

"Let's keep this between us, okay?" and he and three speechless friends left the room.

For weeks after that day I was puzzled. Oh, of course I was exuberant. But my joy was peppered with mystery. Everywhere I went I saw his face. His look followed me. Even as I write this, I can see it.

Head cocked just a bit. Tender twinkle of anticipation under bushy brows. That look that whispered, "Come here. I've got a secret."

And now I know where I'd seen it before. In fact I've seen it again—several times.

I saw it in the eyes of the cancer patient I visited yesterday. Bald from chemotherapy. Shadowed eyes from the disease. Her skin was soft and her hand bony. She recognized me when she awoke. She didn't even say hello. She just lofted her eyebrows, sparkled that sparkle, and said, "I'm ready, Wallace. I'm ready to go."

I saw it last week as I spoke at a funeral. The widower, a wrinkled-faced man with white hair and bifocals. He didn't weep like the others. In fact, at one point I think I saw him smile. I shook his hand afterwards. "Don't worry about me," he exclaimed. Then he motioned for me to lean down so he could say something in my ear. "I know where she is."

But it was this morning that I saw it the clearest. I'd wanted to ask her for days, but the right moment never came. This morning it did. At the breakfast table, just the two of us, she with her cereal, I with my paper, I turned to my daughter and asked her. "Princess?"

"Uh huh?"

"What was it like?"

"What?"

"While you were gone. What was it like?"

She didn't say anything. She just turned her head slightly and looked out the window. When she turned around again, the sparkle was there. She opened her mouth and then closed it, then opened it again. "It's a secret, Dad. A secret too good for words."

Peace where there should be pain. Confidence in the midst of crisis. Hope defying despair. That's what that look says. It is a look that knows the answer to the question asked by every mortal, "Does death have the last word?" I can see Jesus wink as he gives the answer. "Not on your life."[1]

FOR REFLECTION AND DISCUSSION

1. "Wallace assured all who inquired that God was a great God. He assured everyone but himself." Why do you think it is hard for "strong" people to show weakness? How is this sometimes a handicap?

2. Do you ever feel that God is not a great as you say he is? Explain.

3. Have you ever reached a point of desperation similar to Wallace's? What happened?

4. What is it about trying circumstances that often bring people to Jesus?

5. Did you notice how Jesus responded to Jairus's request for help? Even though he was busy, Jesus didn't hesitate. How receptive are you to cries for help? Do your friends see you as a caring and compassionate person—someone they can call on if they are in need? Whom do you feel free to call on? Ask those people if they feel the same toward you, and why.

Chapter 19

RICH YOUNG RULER

Now a man came up to Jesus and asked, "Teacher, what good thing must I do to get eternal life?"

"Why do you ask me about what is good?" Jesus replied. "There is only One who is good. If you want to enter life, obey the commandments."

"Which ones?" the man inquired.

Jesus replied, "'Do not murder, do not commit adultery, do not steal, do not give false testimony, honor your father and mother,' and 'love your neighbor as yourself.'"

"All these I have kept," the young man said. "What do I still lack?"

Jesus answered, "If you want to be perfect, go, sell your possessions and give to the poor, and you will have treasure in heaven. Then come, follow me."

When the young man heard this, he went away sad, because he had great wealth.

Then Jesus said to his disciples, "I tell you the truth, it is hard for a rich man to enter the kingdom of heaven. Again I tell you, it is easier for a camel to go through the eye of a needle than for a rich man to enter the kingdom of God."

When the disciples heard this, they were greatly astonished and asked, "Who then can be saved?"

Jesus looked at them and said, "With man this is impossible, but with God all things are possible."

{ MATT. 19:16–26 NIV }

THE AFFLUENT POOR

We could begin with Sarai laughing. Her wrinkled face buried in bony hands. Her shoulders shaking. Her lungs wheezing. She knows she shouldn't laugh; it's not kosher to laugh at what God says. But just as she catches her breath and wipes away the tears, she thinks about it again—and a fresh wave of hilarity doubles her over.

We could begin with Peter staring. It's a stunned stare. His eyes are the size of grapefruits. He's oblivious to the fish piled to his knees and to the water lapping over the edge of the boat. He's deaf to the demands that he snap out of it and help. Peter is numb, absorbed in one thought—a thought too zany to say aloud.

We could begin with Paul resting. For three days he has wrestled; now he rests. He sits on the floor, in the corner. His face is haggard. His stomach is empty.

His lips are parched. Bags droop beneath the blinded eyes. But there is a slight smile on his lips. A fresh stream is flowing into a stagnant pool, and the water is sweet.

But let's not begin with these. Let's begin elsewhere.

Let's begin with the New Testament yuppie negotiating.

He's rich. Italian shoes. Tailored suit. His money is invested. His plastic is golden. He lives like he flies—first class.

He's young. He pumps away fatigue at the gym and slam-dunks old age on the court. His belly is flat, his eyes sharp. Energy is his trademark, and death is an eternity away.

He's powerful. If you don't think so, just ask him. You got questions? He's got answers. You got problems? He's got solutions. You got dilemmas? He's got opinions. He knows where he's going, and he'll be there tomorrow. He's the new generation. So the old had better pick up the pace or pack their bags.

He has mastered the three "Ps" of yuppiedom. Prosperity. Posterity. Power. He's the rich . . . young . . . ruler.[1]

Till today, life for him has been a smooth cruise down a neon avenue. But today he has a question. A casual concern or a genuine fear? We don't know. We do know he has come for some advice.

For one so used to calling the shots, calling on this carpenter's son for help must be awkward. For a man of his pedigree to seek the counsel of a country rube is not standard procedure. But this is no standard question.

"Teacher," he asks, "what good thing must I do to get eternal life?" The wording of his question betrays his misunderstanding. He thinks he can get eternal life as he gets everything else—by his own strength.

"What must I do?"

What are the requirements, Jesus? What's the break-even point? No need for chitchat; go straight to the bottom line. How much do I need to invest to be certain of my return?

Jesus' answer is intended to make him wince. "If you want to enter life, obey the commandments."

A man with half a conscience would have thrown up his hands at that point. "Keep the commandments? Keep the commandments! Do you know how many commandments there are? Have you read the Law lately? I've tried—honestly, I've tried—but I can't."

That is what the ruler should say, but confession is the farthest thing from his mind. Instead of asking for help, he grabs a pencil and paper and asks for the list.

"Which ones?" He licks his pencil and arches an eyebrow.

Jesus indulges him. "Do not murder, do not commit adultery, do not steal, do not give false testimony, honor your father and mother, and love your neighbor as yourself."

"Great!" thinks the yuppie as he finishes the notes. "Now I've got the quiz. Let's see if I pass.

"Murder? Of course not. Adultery? Well, nothing any red-blooded boy wouldn't do. Stealing? A little extortion, but all justifiable. False testimony? Hmmmm . . . let's move on. Honor your father and mother? Sure, I see them on holidays. Love your neighbor as yourself . . . ?

"Hey," he grins, "a piece of cake. I've done all of these. In fact, I've done them since I was a kid." He swaggers a bit and hooks a thumb in his belt. "Got any other commandments you want to run past me?"

How Jesus keeps from laughing—or crying—is beyond me. The question that was intended to show the ruler how he falls short only convinces him that he stands tall. He's a child dripping water on the floor while telling his mom he hasn't been in the rain.

Jesus gets to the point. "If you want to be perfect, then go sell your possessions and give to the poor, and you will have treasure in heaven."

The statement leaves the young man distraught and the disciples bewildered.

Their question could be ours: "Who then can be saved?"

Jesus' answer shell-shocks the listeners, "With man this is impossible . . ."

Impossible.

He doesn't say improbable. He doesn't say unlikely. He doesn't even say it will be tough. He says it is "impossible." No chance. No way. No loopholes. No hope. Impossible. It's impossible to swim the Pacific. It's impossible to go to the moon on the tail of a kite. You can't climb Mount Everest with a picnic basket and a walking stick. And unless somebody does something, you don't have a chance of going to heaven.

Does that strike you as cold? All your life you've been rewarded according to your performance. You get grades according to your study. You get commendations according to your success. You get money in response to your work.

That's why the rich young ruler thought heaven was just a payment away. It only made sense. You work hard, you pay your dues, and "zap"— your account is credited as paid in full. Jesus says, "No way." What you want costs far more than what you can pay. You don't need a system, you need a Savior. You don't need a resume, you need a Redeemer. For "what is impossible with men is possible with God" (Luke 18:27 NIV).

Don't miss the thrust of this verse: You cannot save yourself. Not through the right rituals. Not through the right doctrine. Not through the right devotion. Not through the right goose bumps. Jesus' point is crystal clear. It is impossible for human beings to save themselves.

You see, it wasn't the money that hindered the rich man; it was the self-sufficiency. It wasn't the possessions; it was the pomp. It wasn't the big bucks; it was the big head. "How hard it is for the rich to enter the kingdom of God!" (Mark 10:23 NIV). It's not just the rich who have difficulty. So do the educated, the strong, the good-looking, the popular, the religious. So do you if you think your piety or power qualifies you as a kingdom candidate.

And if you have trouble digesting what Jesus said to the rich young ruler, then his description of the judgment day will stick in your throat.

It's a prophetic picture of the final day: "Many will say to me on that day, 'Lord, Lord, did we not prophesy in your name, and in your name drive out demons and perform many miracles?'" (Matt. 7:22 NIV).

Astounding. These people are standing before the throne of God and bragging about themselves. The great trumpet has sounded, and they are still tooting their own horns. Rather than sing his praises, they sing their own. Rather than worship God, they read their résumés. When they should be speechless, they speak. In the very aura of the King they boast of self. What is worse—their arrogance or their blindness?

You don't impress the officials at NASA with a paper airplane. You don't boast about your crayon sketches in the presence of Picasso. You don't claim equality with Einstein because you can write "H_2O."

And you don't boast about your goodness in the presence of the Perfect.

"Then I will tell them plainly, 'I never knew you. Away from me, you evildoers'" (Matt. 7:23 NIV).

Mark it down. God does not save us because of what we've done. Only a puny god could be bought with tithes. Only an egotistical god would be impressed with our pain. Only a temperamental god could be satisfied by sacrifices. Only a heartless god would sell salvation to the highest bidders.

And only a great God does for his children what they can't do for themselves.

That is the message of Paul: "For what the law was powerless to do . . . God did" (Rom. 8:3 NIV).

And that is the message of the first beatitude from Christ's Sermon on the Mount. "Blessed are the poor in spirit, for theirs is the kingdom of heaven."

The jewel of joy is given to the impoverished spirits, not the affluent.[2] God's delight is received upon surrender, not awarded upon conquest. The first step to joy is a plea for help, an acknowledgment of moral destitution, an admission of inward paucity. Those who taste God's presence have declared spiritual bankruptcy and are aware of their spiritual crisis. Their cupboards are bare. Their pockets are empty. Their options are gone. They have long since stopped demanding justice; they are pleading for mercy.[3]

They don't brag; they beg.

They ask God to do for them what they can't do without him. They have seen how holy God is and how sinful they are and have agreed with Jesus' statement, "Salvation is impossible."

Oh, the irony of God's delight—born in the parched soil of destitution rather than the fertile ground of achievement.

It's a different path, a path we're not accustomed to taking. We don't often declare our impotence. Admission of failure is not usually admission into joy. Complete confession is not commonly followed by total pardon. But then again, God has never been governed by what is common.

FOR REFLECTION AND DISCUSSION

1. How does this chapter interpret being "poor in spirit"? How does this compare with any previous ideas you had about what this beatitude means?
2. Read Luke 6:20, 24. Luke's version of this beatitude omits the "in spirit" idea entirely; it simply states that "the rich" have their reward here and therefore cannot expect a reward in heaven.
3. Now read Matthew 19:23–24. Jesus tells the rich young ruler directly that "it is hard for a rich man to enter the kingdom of heaven." Do you think the first beatitude applies especially to those who are poor in material possessions? If not, why does Matthew make these specific comments about material wealth?
4. What do you think are the motives behind the rich young ruler's self-justification and overachievement? What is the difference between trying to achieve salvation and trying to please God? Between being poor in spirit and being a poor steward of your God-given gifts?
5. "Those who taste God's presence have declared spiritual bankruptcy and are aware of their spiritual crisis." Have you ever declared yourself spiritually bankrupt? If so, have you asked God to do for you what you can't do without him? If you haven't, wouldn't now be a good time?

Chapter 20

☙

SARAH, PETER,
AND PAUL

Then the LORD said, "I will surely return to you about this time next year, and Sarah your wife will have a son."

Now Sarah was listening at the entrance to the tent, which was behind him. Abraham and Sarah were already old and well advanced in years, and Sarah was past the age of childbearing. So Sarah laughed to herself as she thought, "After I am worn out and my master is old, will I now have this pleasure?"

{ GEN. 18:10–12 NIV }

When he had finished speaking, he said to Simon, "Put out into deep water, and let down the nets for a catch."

Simon answered, "Master, we've worked hard all night and haven't caught anything. But because you say so, I will let down the nets."

When they had done so, they caught such a large number of fish that their nets began to break. So they signaled their partners in the other boat to come and help them, and they came and filled both boats so full that they began to sink.

{ LUKE 5:4–7 NIV }

Meanwhile, Saul was still breathing out murderous threats against the Lord's disciples. He went to the high priest and asked him for letters to the synagogues in Damascus, so that if he found any there who belonged to the Way, whether men or women, he might take them as prisoners to Jerusalem. As he neared Damascus on his journey, suddenly a light from heaven flashed around him. He fell to the ground and heard a voice say to him, "Saul, Saul, why do you persecute me?"

"Who are you, Lord?" Saul asked.

"I am Jesus, whom you are persecuting," he replied. "Now get up and go into the city, and you will be told what you must do."

{ ACTS 9:1–6 NIV }

THE KINGDOM OF
THE ABSURD

The kingdom of heaven. Its citizens are drunk on wonder.

Consider the case of Sarai.[1] She is in her golden years, but God promises her a son. She gets excited. She visits the maternity shop and buys a few dresses. She plans her shower and remodels her tent . . . but no son. She eats a few birthday cakes and blows out a lot of candles . . . still no son. She goes through a decade of wall calendars . . . still no son.

So Sarai decides to take matters into her own hands. ("Maybe God needs me to take care of this one.")

She convinces Abram that time is running out. ("Face it, Abe, you ain't getting any younger, either.") She commands her maid, Hagar, to go into Abram's tent and see if he needs anything. ("And I mean 'anything'!") Hagar goes in a maid. She comes out a mom. And the problems begin.

Hagar is haughty. Sarai is jealous. Abram is dizzy from the dilemma. And God calls the baby boy a "wild donkey"—an appropriate name for one born out of stubbornness and destined to kick his way into history.

It isn't the cozy family Sarai expected. And it isn't a topic Abram and Sarai bring up very often at dinner.

Finally, fourteen years later, when Abram is pushing a century of years and Sarai ninety . . . when Abram has stopped listening to Sarai's advice, and Sarai has stopped giving it . . . when the wallpaper in the nursery is faded and the baby furniture is several seasons out of date . . . when the topic of the promised child brings sighs and tears and long looks into a silent sky . . . God pays them a visit and tells them they had better select a name for their new son.

Abram and Sarai have the same response: laughter. They laugh partly because it is too good to happen and partly because it might. They laugh because they have given up hope, and hope born anew is always funny before it is real.

They laugh at the lunacy of it all.

Abram looks over at Sarai—toothless and snoring in her rocker, head back and mouth wide open, as fruitful as a pitted prune and just as wrinkled. And he cracks up. He tries to contain it, but he can't. He has always been a sucker for a good joke.

Sarai is just as amused. When she hears the news, a cackle escapes before she can contain it. She mumbles something about her husband's needing a lot more than what he's got and then laughs again.

They laugh because that is what you do when someone says he can do the impossible. They laugh a little *at* God, and a lot *with* God—for God is laughing, too. Then, with the smile still on his face, he gets busy doing what he does best—the unbelievable.

He changes a few things—beginning with their names. Abram, the father of one, will now be Abraham, the father of a multitude. Sarai, the barren one, will now be Sarah, the mother.

But their names aren't the only things God changes. He changes their minds. He changes their faith. He changes the number of their tax deductions. He changes the way they define the word *impossible*.

But most of all, he changes Sarah's attitude about trusting God. Were she to hear Jesus' statement about being poor in spirit, she could give a testimony: "He's right. I do things my way, I get a headache. I let God take over, I get a son. You try to figure that out. All I know is I am the first lady in town to pay her pediatrician with a Social Security check."

TWO THOUSAND YEARS LATER, here's another testimony[2]:

"The last thing I wanted to do was fish. But that was exactly what Jesus wanted to do. I had fished all night. My arms ached. My eyes burned.

My neck was sore. All I wanted was to go home and let my wife rub the knots out of my back.

"It had been a long night. I don't know how many times we had thrown that net into the blackness and heard it slap against the sea. I don't know how many times we had held the twine rope as the net sank into the water. All night we had waited for that bump, that tug, that jerk that would clue us to haul in the catch . . . but it had never come. At daybreak, I was ready to go home.

"Just as I was about to leave the beach, I noticed a crowd coming toward me. They were following a lanky fellow who walked with a broad swing and wide gait. He saw me and called my name. 'Morning, Jesus!' I called back. Though he was a hundred yards away, I could see his white smile. 'Quite a crowd, eh?' he yelled, motioning at the mass behind him. I nodded and sat down to watch.

"He stopped near the edge of the water and began to speak. Though I couldn't hear much, I could see a lot. I could see more and more people coming. With all the pressing and shoving, it's a wonder Jesus didn't get pushed down into the water. He was already knee-deep when he looked at me.

"I didn't have to think twice. He climbed into my boat, and John and I followed. We pushed out a bit. I leaned back against the bow, and Jesus began to teach.

"It seemed that half of Israel was on the beach. Men had left their work, women their household chores. I even recognized some priests. How they all listened! They scarcely moved, yet their eyes danced as if they were in some way seeing what they could be.

"When Jesus finished, he turned to me. I stood and had begun to pull anchor when he said, 'Push out into the deep, Peter. Let's fish.'

"I groaned. I looked at John. We were thinking the same thing. As long as he wanted to use the boat for a platform, that was fine. But to use it for a fishing boat—that was our territory. I started to tell this carpenter-teacher,

'You stick to preaching, and I'll stick to fishing.' But I was more polite: 'We worked all night. We didn't catch a thing.'

"He just looked at me. I looked at John. John was waiting for my cue . . .

"I wish I could say I did it because of love. I wish I could say I did it out of devotion. But I can't. All I can say is there is a time to question and a time to listen. So, as much with a grunt as with a prayer, we pushed out.

"With every stroke of the oar, I muttered. With every pull of the paddle, I grumbled. 'No way. No way. Impossible. I may not know much, but I know fishing. And all we're going to come back with are some wet nets.'

"The noise on the beach grew distant, and soon the only sound was the smack of the waves against the hull. Finally we cast anchor. I picked up the heavy netting, held it waist-high, and started to throw it. That's when I caught a glimpse of Jesus out of the corner of my eye. His expression stopped me in midmotion.

"He was leaning out over the edge of the boat, looking out into the water where I was about to throw the net. And, get this, he was smiling. A boyish grin pushed his cheeks high and turned his round eyes into half-moons—the kind of smile you see when a child gives a gift to a friend and watches as it is unwrapped.

"He noticed me looking at him, and he tried to hide the smile, but it persisted. It pushed at the corners of his mouth until a flash of teeth appeared. He had given me a gift and could scarcely contain himself as I opened it.

"'Boy, is he in for a disappointment,' I thought as I threw the net. It flew high, spreading itself against the blue sky and floating down until it flopped against the surface, then sank. I wrapped the rope once around my hand and sat back for the long wait.

"But there was no wait. The slack rope yanked taut and tried to pull me overboard. I set my feet against the side of the boat and yelled for help. John and Jesus sprang to my side.

"We got the net in just before it began to tear. I'd never seen such a catch. It was like plopping down a sack of rocks in the boat. We began to take in water. John screamed for the other boat to help us.

"It was quite a scene: four fishermen in two boats, knee-deep in fish, and one carpenter seated on our bow, relishing the pandemonium.

"That's when I realized who he was. And that's when I realized who I was: I was the one who told God what he couldn't do!

"'Go away from me, Lord; I'm a sinful man.' There wasn't anything else I could say.

"I don't know what he saw in me, but he didn't leave. Maybe he thought if I would let him tell me how to fish, I would let him tell me how to live.

"It was a scene I would see many times over the next couple of years—in cemeteries with the dead, on hillsides with the hungry, in storms with the frightened, on roadsides with the sick. The characters would change, but the theme wouldn't. When we would say, 'No way,' he would say, 'My way.' Then the ones who doubted would scramble to salvage the blessing. And the One who gave it would savor the surprise."

"My power shows up best in weak people" (2 Cor. 12:9 TLB).

God said those words. Paul wrote them down. God said he was looking for empty vessels more than strong muscles. Paul proved it.

Before he encountered Christ, Paul had been somewhat of a hero among the Pharisees. You might say he was their Wyatt Earp. He kept the law and order—or, better said, revered the Law and gave the orders. Good Jewish moms held him up as an example of a good Jewish boy. He was given the seat of honor at the Jerusalem Lions' Club Wednesday luncheon. He had a "Who's Who in Judaism" paperweight on his desk and was selected "Most Likely to Succeed" by his graduating class. He was quickly establishing himself as the heir apparent to his teacher, Gamaliel.

If there is such a thing as a religious fortune, Paul had it. He was a spiritual billionaire, born with one foot in heaven, and he knew it:

If anyone ever had reason to hope that he could save himself, it would be I. If others could be saved by what they are, certainly I could! For I went through the Jewish initiation ceremony when I was eight days old, having been born into a pure-blooded Jewish home that was a branch of the old original Benjamin family. So I was a real Jew if there ever was one! What's more, I was a member of the Pharisees who demand the strictest obedience to every Jewish law and custom. And sincere? Yes, so much so that I greatly persecuted the church; and I tried to obey every Jewish rule and regulation down to the very last point. (Phil. 3:4–6 TLB).

Blue-blooded and wild-eyed, this young zealot was hell-bent on keeping the kingdom pure—and that meant keeping the Christians out. He marched through the countryside like a general demanding that backslidden Jews salute the flag of the motherland or kiss their family and hopes good-bye.

All this came to a halt, however, on the shoulder of a highway. Equipped with subpoenas, handcuffs, and a posse, Paul was on his way to do a little personal evangelism in Damascus. That's when someone slammed on the stadium lights, and he heard the voice.

When he found out whose voice it was, his jaw hit the ground, and his body followed. He braced himself for the worst. He knew it was all over. He felt the noose around his neck. He smelled the flowers in the hearse. He prayed that death would be quick and painless.

But all he got was silence and the first of a lifetime of surprises.

He ended up bewildered and befuddled in a borrowed bedroom. God left him there a few days with scales on his eyes so thick that the only direction he could look was inside himself. And he didn't like what he saw.

He saw himself for what he really was—to use his own words, the worst of sinners (1 Tim.1:15 NIV). A legalist. A killjoy. A bumptious braggart who claimed to have mastered God's code. A dispenser of justice who weighed salvation on a panscale.

That's when Ananias found him. He wasn't much to look at—haggard and groggy after three days of turmoil. Sarai wasn't much to look at either, nor was Peter. But what the three have in common says more than a volume of systematic theology. For when they gave up, God stepped in, and the result was a roller-coaster ride straight into the kingdom.

Paul was a step ahead of the rich young ruler. He knew better than to strike a deal with God. He didn't make any excuses; he just pleaded for mercy. Alone in the room with his sins on his conscience and blood on his hands, he asked to be cleansed.

Ananias' instructions to Paul are worth reading: "What are you waiting for? Get up, be baptized and wash your sins away, calling on his name" (Acts 22:16 NIV).

He didn't have to be told twice. The legalist Saul was buried, and the liberator Paul was born. He was never the same afterwards. And neither was the world.

Stirring sermons, dedicated disciples, and six thousand miles of trails. If his sandals weren't slapping, his pen was writing. If he wasn't explaining the mystery of grace, he was articulating the theology that would determine the course of Western civilization.

All of his words could be reduced to one sentence. "We preach Christ crucified" (1 Cor. 1:23 NIV). It wasn't that he lacked other sermon outlines; it was just that he couldn't exhaust the first one.

The absurdity of the whole thing kept him going. Jesus should have finished him on the road. He should have left him for the buzzards. He should have sent him to hell. But he didn't. He sent him to the lost.

Paul himself called it crazy. He described it with phrases like "stumbling block" and "foolishness," but chose in the end to call it "grace" (1 Cor. 1:23; Eph. 2:8 NIV).

And he defended his unquenchable loyalty by saying, "The love of Christ leaves [me] no choice" (2 Cor. 5:14 NEB).

Paul never took a course in missions. He never sat in on a committee meeting. He never read a book on church growth. He was just inspired by the Holy Spirit and punch-drunk on the love that makes the impossible possible: salvation.

The message is gripping: Show a man his failures without Jesus, and the result will be found in the roadside gutter. Give a man religion without reminding him of his filth, and the result will be arrogance in a three-piece suit. But get the two in the same heart—get sin to meet Savior and Savior to meet sin—and the result just might be another Pharisee turned preacher who sets the world on fire.

FOUR PEOPLE: THE RICH young ruler, Sarah, Peter, Paul. A curious thread strings the four together—their names.

The final three had their names changed—Sarai to Sarah, Simon to Peter, Saul to Paul. But the first one, the young yuppie, is never mentioned by name.

Perhaps that's the clearest explanation of the first beatitude. The one who made a name for himself is nameless. But the ones who called on Jesus' name—and his name only—got new names and, even more, new life.

For Reflection and Discussion

1. Why is being poor in spirit as described in these last two chapters so difficult for most of us? Why do we have such a hard time admitting our own inadequacy and failures, even to God and ourselves?

2. List what you consider your five greatest strengths and your five greatest weaknesses. Does being poor in spirit mean denying your strengths or not trying to improve your weaknesses? Does it mean being "down on yourself"? Why or why not?

3. Read the following parables describing the "kingdom of heaven": Matthew 13:24–33, 44–50. What additional insight do these parables give about the nature of the "kingdom" in which the poor in spirit will live?

4. Read Matthew 16:13–20, which tells the circumstances under which Peter's name was changed and he was given the "keys to the kingdom of heaven." What elements of this account point to Peter's being poor in spirit? What does this passage tell you about the nature of the kingdom?

5. When Sarah, Peter, and Paul said, "No way," God would say, "My way." Has this ever happened to you? If so, explain.

Chapter 21

❧

LAZARUS

A man named Lazarus was sick. He lived in the town of Bethany, where Mary and her sister Martha lived. Mary was the woman who later put perfume on the Lord and wiped his feet with her hair. Mary's brother was Lazarus, the man who was now sick. So Mary and Martha sent someone to tell Jesus, "Lord, the one you love is sick." . . .

When Jesus arrived, he learned that Lazarus had already been dead and in the tomb for four days. Bethany was about two miles from Jerusalem. Many of the Jews had come there to comfort Martha and Mary about their brother. . . .

Martha said to Jesus, "Lord, if you had been here, my brother would not have died. But I know that even now God will give you anything you ask."

Jesus said, "Your brother will rise and live again." . . .

When Jesus saw Mary crying and the Jews who came with her also crying, he was upset and was deeply troubled. He asked, "Where did you bury him?"

"Come and see, Lord," they said.

Jesus cried. . . .

Again feeling very upset, Jesus came to the tomb. It was a cave with a large stone covering the entrance. Jesus said, "Move the stone away."

Martha, the sister of the dead man, said, "But, Lord, it has been four days since he died. There will be a bad smell."

Then Jesus said to her, "Didn't I tell you that if you believed you would see the glory of God?"

So they moved the stone away from the entrance. Then Jesus looked up and said, "Father, I thank you that you heard me. I know that you always hear me, but I said these things because of the people here around me. I want them to believe that you sent me." After Jesus said this, he cried out in a loud voice, "Lazarus, come out!" The dead man came out, his hands and feet wrapped with pieces of cloth, and a cloth around his face.

Jesus said to them, "Take the cloth off of him and let him go."

{ JOHN 11:1-3, 17-19, 20-23, 33-35, 38-44 }

THE FINAL WITNESS

John doesn't tell us everything Jesus did. But he tells us those acts that will lead us to faith. John selects seven miracles. He begins softly with the quiet miracle of water to wine and then crescendos to the public resurrection of Lazarus. Seven miracles are offered, and seven witnesses are examined, each one building on the testimony of the previous.

Let's see if we can feel their full impact.

Pretend you are in a courtroom, a nearly empty courtroom. Present are four people: a judge, a lawyer, an orphan, and a would-be guardian. The judge is God, Jesus is the one who seeks to be the guardian, and you are the orphan. You have no name, no inheritance, no home. The lawyer is proposing that you be placed in Jesus' care.

Who is the lawyer? A Galilean fisherman by the name of John.

He has presented the court with six witnesses. It is time for the seventh. But before calling him to the stand, the lawyer reviews the case. "We started this case with the wedding in Cana." He paces as he speaks, measuring each word. "They had no wine, none at all. But when Jesus spoke, water became wine. The best wine. Delicious wine. You heard the testimony of the wedding attendants. They saw it happen."

He pauses, then moves on. "Then we heard the words of the foreign official. His son was nearly dead."

You nod. You remember the man's testimony. Articulate, he had spoken of how he had called every doctor and tried every treatment, but nothing had helped his son. Just when he was about to give up hope, someone told him about a healer in Galilee.

Through his thickened accent the dignitary had explained, "I had no other choice. I went to him out of desperation. Look! Look what the teacher did for my son." The boy had stood, and you had stared. It was hard to believe such a healthy youngster had ever been near death.

You listen intently as John continues, "And, your honor, don't forget the crippled man near the pool. For thirty-eight years he had not walked. But then Jesus came and, well, the court saw him. Remember? We saw him walk into this room. We heard his story.

"And, as if that was not enough, we also heard the testimony of the boy with the lunch. He was part of a crowd of thousands who had followed Jesus in order to hear him teach and to see him heal. Just when the little boy was about to open his lunch basket to eat, he was asked to bring it to Jesus. One minute it held a lunch; the next it held a feast."

John pauses again, letting the silence of the courtroom speak. No one can deny these testimonies. The judge listens. The lawyer listens. And you, the orphan, say nothing.

"Then there was the storm. Peter described it to us. The boat bouncing on the waves. Thunder. Lightning. Storms like that can kill. I know. I used to make a living on a boat! Peter's testimony about what happened was true. I was there. The Master walked on the water. And the moment he stepped into the boat, we were safe."

John pauses again. Sunlight squared by a window makes a box on the floor. John steps into the box. "Then, yesterday, you met a man who had never seen light. His world was dark. Black. He was blind. Blind from birth."

John pauses and dramatically states what the man born blind had said: "Jesus healed my eyes."

Six testimonies have been given. Six miracles have been verified. John gestures toward the table where sit the articles of evidence: The water jugs that held the wine. The signed affidavit of the doctor who'd treated the sick son. The cot of the cripple, the basket of the boy. Peter had brought a broken oar to show the strength of the storm. And the blind man had left his cup and cane. He didn't need to beg anymore.

"And now," John says, turning to the judge, "we have one final witness to call and one more piece of evidence to submit."

He goes to his table and returns with a white linen sheet. You lean forward, unsure of what he is holding. "This is a burial shroud," he explains. Placing the clothing on the table he requests, "Your honor permitting, I call our final witness to the chair, Lazarus of Bethany."

Heavy courtroom doors open, and a tall man enters. He strides down the aisle and pauses before Jesus long enough to place a hand on his shoulder and say, "Thank you." You can hear the tenderness in his voice. Lazarus then turns and takes his seat in the witness chair.

"State your name for the court."

"Lazarus."

"Have you heard of a man called Jesus of Nazareth?"

"Who hasn't?"

"How do you know him?"

"He is my friend. We, my sisters and I, have a house in Bethany. When he comes to Jerusalem, he often stays with us. My sisters, Mary and Martha, have become believers in him as well."

"Believers?"

"Believers that he is the Messiah. The Son of God."

"Why do you believe that?"

Lazarus smiles. "How could I not believe? I was dead. I had been dead for four days. I was in the tomb. I was prayed for and buried. I was dead. But Jesus called me out of the grave."

"Tell us what happened."

"Well, I've always been sickly. That's why I've stayed with my sisters, you know. They care for me. My heart never has been the strongest, so I have to be careful. Martha, the oldest sister, she's, well, she's like a mother to me. It was Martha who called Jesus when my heart failed."

"Is that when you died?"

"No, but almost. I lingered for a few days. But I knew I was near the edge. The doctors would just come in and shake their heads and walk out. I had one sandal in the grave."

"Is that when Jesus came?"

"No, we kept hoping he would. Martha would sit by the bed at night, and she would whisper over and over and over, 'Be strong, Lazarus. Jesus will be here any minute.' We just knew he would come. I mean, he had healed all those strangers; surely he would heal me. I was his friend."

"What delayed him?"

"For the longest time we didn't know. I thought he might be in prison or something. I kept waiting and waiting. Every day I got weaker. My vision faded, and I couldn't see. I drifted in and out. Every time someone entered my room, I thought it might be him. But it never was. He never came."

"Were you angry?"

"More confused than angry. I just didn't understand."

"Then what happened?"

"Well, I woke up one night. My chest was so tight I could hardly breathe. I must have sat up because Martha and Mary came to my bed. They took my hand. I heard them calling my name, but then I began to fall. It was like a dream, I was falling, spinning wildly in midair. Their voices grew fainter and fainter and then nothing. The spinning stopped, the falling stopped. And the hurting stopped. I was at peace."

"At peace?"

"Like I was asleep. Resting. Tranquil. I was dead."

"Then what happened?"

"Well, Martha can tell the details. The funeral was planned. The family came. Friends traveled from Jerusalem. They buried me."

"Did Jesus come to the funeral?"

"No."

"He still wasn't there?"

"No, when he heard I was buried, he waited an extra four days."

"Why?"

Lazarus stopped and looked at Jesus. "To make his point."

John smiled knowingly.

"What happened next?"

"I heard his voice."

"Whose voice?"

"The voice of Jesus."

"But I thought you were dead."

"I was."

"I, uh, thought you were in a grave."

"I was."

"How does a dead man in a grave hear the voice of a man?"

"He doesn't. The dead hear only the voice of God. I heard the voice of God."

"What did he say?"

"He didn't say it; he shouted it."

"What did he shout?"

"'Lazarus, come out!'"

"And you heard him?"

"As if he were in the tomb with me. My eyes opened; my fingers moved. I lifted my head. I was alive again. I heard the stone being rolled away. The light poured in. It took a minute for my eyes to adjust."

"What did you see?"

"A circle of faces looking in at me."

"Then what did you do?"

"I stood up. Jesus gave me his hand and pulled me out. He told the people to get me some real clothes, and they did."

"So you died, were in the tomb four days, then Jesus called you back to life? Were there any witnesses to this?"

Lazarus chuckles. "Only a hundred or so."

"That's all, Lazarus, thank you. You may step down."

John returns to the judge. "You have heard the testimonies. I now leave the decision in your hands." With that he returns to the table and takes his seat. The guardian stands. He doesn't identify himself. He doesn't need to. All recognize him. He is Jesus Christ.

Jesus' voice fills the courtroom. "I represent an orphan who is the sum of all you have seen. Like the party that had no wine, this one has no cause for celebration. Like the dignitary's son, this child is spiritually ill. Like the cripple and the beggar, he can't walk and is blind. He is starving, but earth has no food to fill him. He faces storms as severe as the one on Galilee, but earth has no compass to guide him. And most of all, he is dead. Just like Lazarus. Dead. Spiritually dead."

"I will do for him what I did for them. I'll give him joy, strength, healing, sight, safety, nourishment, new life. All are his. If you will permit."

The judge speaks his answer. "You are my Son, whom I love, and I am very pleased with you" (Luke 3:22). God looks at you. "I will permit it," he says, "on one condition. That the orphan request it."

John has presented the witnesses.

The witnesses have told their stories.

The Master has offered to do for you what he did for them. He will bring wine to your table, sight to your eyes, strength for your step and, most of all, power over your grave. He will do for you what he did for them.

The Judge has given his blessing. The rest is up to you.

Now the choice is yours.

FOR REFLECTION AND DISCUSSION

1. "'The dead hear only the voice of God . . .,' said Lazarus . . . 'I heard the voice of God.'" If a man is dead, how can he hear anything? How did Lazarus know it was the voice of God he heard? In what way do "dead men" still hear the voice of God today?

2. "Jesus said . . . 'I'll give him joy, strength, healing, sight, safety, nourishment, new life.'" Does Jesus still give us these gifts today? If so, how?

3. Which of the gifts listed above means the most to you? Explain your choice.

4. Read John 20:20–31. What was the purpose of writing down Jesus' miracles? Have they had this intended effect on you? Why or why not?

5. Read Ephesians 2:1–5. How could we be described in our pre-Christian days, according to verses 1–3? How was our status changed as described in verses 4–5? What prompted this change in status?

Chapter 22

❧

PETER

When the Sabbath was over, Mary Magdalene, Mary the mother of James, and Salome bought spices so that they might go to anoint Jesus' body. Very early on the first day of the week, just after sunrise, they were on their way to the tomb and they asked each other, "Who will roll the stone away from the entrance of the tomb?"

But when they looked up, they saw that the stone, which was very large, had been rolled away. As they entered the tomb, they saw a young man dressed in a white robe sitting on the right side, and they were alarmed.

"Don't be alarmed," he said. "You are looking for Jesus the Nazarene, who was crucified. He has risen! He is not here. See the place where they laid him. But go, tell his disciples and Peter, 'He is going ahead of you into Galilee. There you will see him, just as he told you.'"

{ MARK 16:1–7 NIV }

The Gospel of the
Second Chance

It was like discovering the prize in a box of Crackerjacks or spotting a little pearl in a box of buttons or stumbling across a ten dollar bill in a drawer full of envelopes.

It was small enough to overlook. Only two words. I know I'd read that passage a hundred times. But I'd never seen it. Maybe I'd passed over it in the excitement of the resurrection. Or, since Mark's account of the resurrection is by far the briefest of the four, maybe I'd just not paid too much attention. Or, maybe since it's in the last chapter of the gospel, my weary eyes had always read too quickly to note this little phrase.

But I won't miss it again. It's highlighted in yellow and underlined in red. You might want to do the same. Look in Mark, chapter 16. Read the first five verses about the women's surprise when they find the stone moved to the side. Then feast on that beautiful phrase spoken by the angel, "He is not here, he is risen," but don't pause for too long. Go a bit further. Get your pencil ready and enjoy this jewel in the seventh verse (here it comes). The verse reads like this: "But go, tell his disciples and Peter that he is going before you to Galilee."

Did you see it? Read it again. (This time I italicized the words.)

"But go, tell his disciples *and Peter* that he is going before you to Galilee."

Now tell me if that's not a hidden treasure.

If I might paraphrase the words, "Don't stay here, go tell the disciples," a pause, then a smile, "and especially tell Peter, that he is going before you to Galilee."

What a line. It's as if all of heaven had watched Peter fall—and it's as if all of heaven wanted to help him back up again. "Be sure and tell Peter that he's not left out. Tell him that one failure doesn't make a flop."

Whew!

No wonder they call it the gospel of the second chance.

Not many second chances exist in the world today. Just ask the kid who didn't make the little league team or the fellow who got the pink slip or the mother of three who got dumped for a "pretty little thing."

Not many second chances. Nowadays it's more like, "It's now or never." "Around here we don't tolerate incompetence." "Gotta get tough to get along." "Not much room at the top." "Three strikes and you're out." "It's a dog-eat-dog world!"

Jesus has a simple answer to our masochistic mania. "It's a dog-eat-dog world?" he would say. "Then don't live with the dogs." That makes sense doesn't it? Why let a bunch of other failures tell you how much of a failure you are?

Sure you can have a second chance.

Just ask Peter. One minute he felt lower than a snake's belly and the next minute he was the high hog at the trough. Even the angels wanted this distraught netcaster to know that it wasn't over. The message came loud and clear from the celestial Throne Room through the divine courier. "Be sure and tell Peter that he gets to bat again."

Those who know these types of things say that the Gospel of Mark is really the transcribed notes and dictated thoughts of Peter. If this is true, then it was Peter himself who included these two words! And if these really are his words, I can't help but imagine that the old fisherman had to brush away a tear and swallow a lump when he got to this point in the story.

It's not every day that you get a second chance. Peter must have known that. The next time he saw Jesus, he got so excited that he barely got his britches on before he jumped into the cold water of the Sea of Galilee. It was also enough, so they say, to cause this backwoods Galilean to carry the gospel of the second chance all the way to Rome where they killed him. If you've ever wondered what would cause a man to be willing to be crucified upside down, maybe now you know.

It's not every day that you find someone who will give you a second chance—much less someone who will give you a second chance every day.

But in Jesus, Peter found both.

For Reflection and Discussion

1. What is meant by the "gospel of the second chance"? What other names could it be given?

2. Of all the followers who deserted Jesus, perhaps Peter's story is the most striking. Read the account of his denial of Jesus in Mark 14:27–31, 66–72 and then the angel's response after Jesus' resurrection in Mark 16:1–7. Also read Luke 24:33–34 and John 21:15–19. What message is conveyed in Peter's being singled out? What seems to be Jesus' attitude toward Peter—frustration, disappointment, concern, love?

3. What do you think is Jesus' attitude about giving you a second chance, or a third chance, or a fourth? Would he do any less for you than for Peter?

4. Can you think of a time you were given a second chance? How did it affect you? How willing are you to offer others a second chance?

5. As a reminder that he is the God of second chances, write out Lamentations 3:19–26 and place it where you can read it every morning.

Conclusion

CAST OF CHARACTERS

They weren't all exactly what you'd call a list of "Who's Who in Purity and Sainthood," were they? In fact, some of their antics and attitudes would make you think of the Saturday night crowd at the county jail. What few halos there are among this cast of characters could probably use a bit of straightening and polishing. Yet, strange as it may seem, it is this very humanness that makes them refreshing. So refreshing that should you ever need a reminder of God's tolerance, you'd find it in these people. If you ever wonder how in the world God could use you to change the world, look at these people.

This ragbag of ne'er-do-wells and has-beens, failed followers and despairing church leaders who found hope, not in their performance, but in God's proverbially open arms.

Remember Abraham, the father of a nation who wasn't without his weaknesses. He had a fibbing tongue that wouldn't stop! One time, in order to save his neck, he let the word get out that Sarah wasn't his wife but his sister, which was only half true (Gen.12:10–20 NIV).

And then, not long later, he did it again! "And there Abraham said of his wife Sarah, 'She is my sister'" (Gen. 20:2 NIV).

Twice he traded in his integrity for security. That's what you call confidence in God's promises? Can you build a nation on that kind of faith? God can. God took what was good and forgave what was bad and used "old forked tongue" to start a nation.

Let's not fail to mention Jonah. God's ambassador to Nineveh. Jonah, however, had other ideas. He had no desire to go to that heathen city. So he hopped on another boat while God wasn't looking (or at least that's what Jonah thought). God put him in a whale's belly to bring him back to his senses. But even the whale couldn't stomach this missionary for too long. A good burp and Jonah went flying over the surf and landed big-eyed and repentant on the beach. (Which just goes to show that you can't keep a good man down.)

And on and on the stories go: Elijah, the prophet who pouted; Solomon, the king who knew too much; Jacob, the wheeler-dealer; Gomer, the prostitute. One story after another of God using man's best and overcoming man's worst.

The reassuring lesson is clear. God used (and uses!) people to change the world. *People!* Not saints or superhumans or geniuses, but people. Crooks, creeps, lovers, and liars—he uses them all. And what they may lack in perfection, God makes up for in love.

Jesus later summarized God's stubborn love with a parable. He told about a teenager who decided that life at the farm was too slow for his tastes. So with pockets full of inheritance money, he set out to find the big time. What he found instead were hangovers, fair-weather friends, and long unemployment lines. When he had had just about as much of the pig's life as he could take, he swallowed his pride, dug his hands deep into his empty pockets, and began the long walk home; all the while rehearsing a speech that he planned to give to his father.

He never used it. Just when he got to the top of the hill, his father, who'd been waiting at the gate, saw him. The boy's words of apology were quickly muffled by the father's words of forgiveness. And the boy's weary body fell into his father's opened arms.

The same open arms welcomed him that had welcomed Abraham, Moses, David, and Jonah. No wagging fingers. No clenched fists. No "I told you so!" slaps or "Where have you been?" interrogations. No crossed arms. No black eyes or fat lips. No. Only sweet, open arms. If you ever wonder how God can use you to make a difference in your world, just look at those he has already used and take heart. Look at the forgiveness found in those open arms and take courage.

And, by the way, never were those arms opened so wide as they were on the Roman cross. One arm extending back into history and the other reaching into the future. An embrace of forgiveness offered for anyone who'll come. A hen gathering her chicks. A father receiving his own. A redeemer redeeming the world. "I am here," he assures, "and with me are the children God has given me" (Heb. 2:13).

FOR REFLECTION AND DISCUSSION

1. Who would you list in a "Who's Who" of the five most outstanding men and women of the Bible other than Jesus? What strengths did each possess? What weaknesses did each possess? How was each person used to change the world?

2. How does God use our weaknesses for his purpose, according to 2 Corinthians 4:7–18 and 2 Corinthians 12:7–10?

3. If Satan were to try to convince you that you were of no special value to the Lord, how might he do it? How would you answer him?

4. You are a significant player in God's "cast of characters." Based on what you've learned through these common people in the hands of an uncommon God, how might you describe your role in God's drama up until now?

5. Looking back at your list of your five greatest strengths (from chapter 20), what do you think God may be calling you to do in the next chapter of your life? Write it down and pray that God will guide and sustain you as you endeavor to use your strengths and weaknesses to change your world.

NOTES

Chapter 2: MATTHEW: FRIEND OF FLOPS

1. Thanks to Landon Saunders for sharing this story with me.

Chapter 4: MEPHIBOSHETH: THE PRIVILEGE OF PAUPERS

1. Dr. Paul Faulkner, *Achieving Success Without Failing Your Family* (W. Monroe, LA: Howard Publishing, 1994), 14–15.
2. *1041 Sermon Illustrations, Ideas and Expositions*, compiled and edited by A. Gordon Nasby (Grand Rapids, MI: Baker, 1953), 244.
3. Charles R. Swindoll, *The Grace Awakening* (Waco, TX: Word, 1990, 2003), 70. Used by permission.

Chapter 7: ABIGAIL: BARBARIC BEHAVIOR

1. Ernest Gordon, *To End All Wars: A True Story About the Will to Survive and the Courage to Forgive* (Grand Rapids, MI: Zondervan, 2002), 105–6, 101.
2. Hans Wilhelm Hertzberg, *1 and 11 Samuel*, trans. J.S. Bowden (Philadelphia: Westminster John Knox Press, 1964), 199–200.
3. Gordon, 101–2.

Chapter 9: JOHN: I CAN TURN YOUR TRAGEDY INTO TRIUMPH

1. Arthur W. Pink, *Exposition of the Gospel of John* (Grand Rapids, MI: Zondervan, 1975), 1077.
2. William Barclay, *The Gospel of John*, vol. 2, rev. ed. (Philadelphia: Westminster Press, 1975), 267.

Chapter 10: PAUL: HIDDEN HEROES

1. See Matthew 11:2.
2. *1,041 Sermon Illustrations, Ideas and Expositions*, 180–81.

Chapter 11: TWO CRIMINALS: I WILL LET YOU CHOOSE

1. Paul Aurandt, *Paul Harvey's the Rest of the Story* (New York: Bantam Press, 1977), 47.

Chapter 14: DAVID: FACING YOUR GIANTS

1. Author's paraphrase.
2. See Exodus 9:22–23; Joshua 6:15–20; 1 Samuel 7:10.
3. Author's paraphrase.
4. Emphasis mine in this list of scriptures.

Chapter 17: NICODEMUS: THE MOST FAMOUS CONVERSATION IN THE BIBLE

1. A colonnade on the east of the temple, so called from a tradition that it was a relic of Solomon's temple left standing after the destruction of Jerusalem by the Babylonians. (See *Bible Encyclopedia*, S.V. "Solomon's Porch," http://www.christiananswers.net/dictionary/porchsolomons.html.)
2. The earliest copies of the books of the New Testament were written in Greek, so Greek word studies shed light on the meaning of New Testament Passages.
3. *The New Testament Greek Lexicon*, S.V. "pa/lin," http://www.searchgodsword.org/lex/grk/view.cgi?number=3825.
4. Ibid., S.V. "anothen," http://www.searchgodsword.org/lex/grk/view.cgi?number=509&1=en.
5. Stanley Barnes, comp., *Sermons on John 3:16* (Greenville, SC: Ambassador Productions, 1999), 90.
6. James Montgomery Boice, *The Gospel of John: An Expositional Commentary* (Grand Rapids, MI: Zondervan Publishing House, 1985), 195.
7. Barnes, 25.

Chapter 18: JAIRUS: THE SPARKLE FROM ETERNITY

1. Based on Mark 5:22–43; Matthew 9:18–26; and Luke 8:41–56.

Chapter 19: RICH YOUNG RULER: THE AFFLUENT POOR

1. His story is told in Matthew 19, Mark 10, and Luke 18.
2. Frederick Dale Bruner clarifies this as he interprets Matthew 5:3: "Blessed are those who feel their poverty . . . and so cry out to heaven." *The*

Christbook: Matthew 1–12 (Waco, TX: Word Publishing, 1987), 135.

3. The word Jesus used for "poor" is a word which, when used in its most basic sense, "would not indicate the pauper, one so poor that he must daily work for his living, but the beggar, one who is dependent upon others for support." William Hendricksen, *Exposition of the Gospel of Matthew* (Grand Rapids, MI: Baker, 1973), 269.

Chapter 20: SARAH, PETER, AND PAUL: THE KINGDOM OF THE ABSURD

1. See Genesis 16–18, 21.

2. See Luke 5.

Sources

The chapters in this book have been taken from the following sources by Max Lucado:

Joseph, Joseph's Prayer: *He Still Moves Stones*
Matthew, Friend of Flops: *Next Door Savior*
Woman Who Washed Jesus' Feet, The 7:47 Principle: *A Love Worth Giving*
Mephibosheth, The Privilege of Paupers: *In the Grip of Grace*
Samaritan Woman, Two Tombstones: *Six Hours One Friday*
Mary, Martha, and Lazarus, Your Place in God's Band: *A Gentle Thunder*
Abigail, Barbaric Behavior: *Facing Your Giants*
Paralyzed Man, Bright Lights on Dark Nights: *He Still Moves Stones*
John, I Can Turn Your Tragedy into Triumph: *He Chose the Nails*
Paul, Hidden Heroes: *When God Whispers Your Name*
Two Criminals, I Will Let You Choose: *He Chose the Nails*
Moses, The Voice from the Mop Bucket: *When God Whispers Your Name*
Joseph, When Crickets Make You Angry: *When God Whispers Your Name*
David, Facing Your Giants: *Facing Your Giants*
Esther, Touching the King's Heart: *The Great House of God*
Job, Where Man Covers His Mouth: *The Great House of God*
Nicodemus, The Most Famous Conversation in the Bible: *3:16*
Jairus, The Sparkle from Eternity: *Six Hours One Friday*
Rich Young Ruler, The Affluent Poor: *The Applause of Heaven*
Sarah, Peter, and Paul, The Kingdom of the Absurd: *The Applause of Heaven*
Lazarus, The Final Witness: *A Gentle Thunder*
Peter, The Gospel of the Second Chance: *No Wonder They Call Him the Savior*